Daniel G.11

Contemporary Politics Series

Introducing Political Science

**Themes and Concepts
in Studying Politics**

Edited by Lynton Robins

**Longman
London and New York**

**The Politics
Association**

LONGMAN GROUP LIMITED
Longman House, Burnt Mill, Harlow, Essex CM20 2JE, UK
and Associated Companies throughout the World.

Published in the United States of America
by Longman Inc., New York

First published 1985
ISBN 0 582 35493 5

Set in 10/12pt. IBM Press Roman
Printed in Great Britain by The Bath Press Ltd.

British Library Cataloguing in Publication Data

Introducing political science: themes and
    concepts in studying politics.
    1. Political science
    I. Robins, Lynton
    320   JA71

    ISBN 0-582-35493-5

Library of Congress Cataloging in Publication Data
Introducing political science.
    Includes bibliographies and index.
    1. Political science — Addresses, essays, lectures.
I. Robins, L. J. (Lynton J.)
JA66.I565 1985   320   85-46

ISBN 0-582-35493-5

Contents

An Introduction to Political Science

Lynton Robins

In recent years there has been a modest revival in the literature dealing with the nature, scope and methods of Political Science. The journal of the Politics Association has contributed to this debate with a series of articles on the various areas and sub-fields which make up the discipline together with annual surveys of course development within higher education.[1] This book, based on articles published in *Teaching Politics,* aims to provide intending students of Political Science with a map charting out the frontiers and boundaries of the discipline. But this is no easy task, since disagreement and conflict exists within the discipline over the way things should be as it does within the activity of politics at large. Sometimes the boundaries between the sub-fields are contested fiercely by rival parties who advocate very different approach roads to their destinations.

Recent books offer little in the way of certainty about the identity of Political Science to newcomers. What emerges from reading accounts such as Jean Blondel, *The Discipline of Politics* (1981), Geoffrey Pontin and Peter Gill, *Introduction to Politics* (1982) or the two books from Adrian Leftwich, *Redefining Politics* (1983) and *What is Politics?* (1984) is that there is relatively little agreement on what Political Science is and consequently considerable confusion over where the boundaries should be drawn and what they should enclose. It is also clear that various antagonists are not clashing only over the relatively technical issues such as the content or methods of the discipline, but are disagreeing on fundamental questions concerning the purpose and role of Political Science in society.

THE STUDENT IN POLITICAL SCIENCE

Most university courses in Political Science include the 'holy trinity' of Political Theory, British Politics and Comparative Politics. Almost all undergraduates explore the political ideas contained in the 'great books' as well as study the political institutions of Britain and one other country. But here any similarities end. Not only will students from different universities have approached the 'holy trinity' in a variety of ways, experiencing different emphases and treatments within each component, but they will have specialised into highly distinctive sub-fields. By the time they have finished, graduates from different educational institutions will find themselves holding degrees in the same discipline but having covered surprisingly little common ground in their studies. Adrian Leftwich pointed to what he calls the 'local academic culture' which gives rise to and perpetuates these differences in approach and emphasis between university departments. It is this local culture which determines the way in which Political Science is defined. He argued that:

> the definition and delimitation of the subject-matter of politics will shape what is taught and, in some respect, how it is taught . . . the conception or conceptions of politics which predominate in a particular department will, for instance, influence the kind of specialist staff that are sought and appointed . . . and in due course will come to influence the composition and balance of the department, and hence what is taught.[2]

Disagreement over the subject-matter of Political Science — what it is appropriate to study — may frustrate the intending student who is seeking simple answers. There is no brief statement along the lines 'Political Science is the study of . . . ' which commands a wide consensus among political scientists. For some the study of politics is about the use of power in governmental institutions; for others it is about the study of power in society at large. To some extent this ambivalence is reflected in the very name of the discipline — which varies from 'Government' and 'Political Theory and Institutions' to 'Politics', 'Political Science' and 'Political Studies'.

What is Political?

One of the central issues, then, which divides political scientists concerns what it is appropriate to study. Let us explore the problem by imagining a typical situation in a university department in which a class of students is attending a lecture on International Relations. This simple situation provides a resource for considering where the limit of 'what is political' might be drawn.

The lecturer is exploring the different strategies of crisis management pursued by Nato and the Warsaw Pact countries. The topic involves concepts such as power, force and deterrence, and explores the values and perceptions of political elites. No political scientist would challenge or deny that this topic had a legitimate place within the discipline. But let us examine the situation more closely.

The number of students attending the class is fewer than in previous years. The number of students that the department was allowed to enrol on to its courses was reduced through an internal university decision which, in turn, reflected government policy of producing more science graduates and fewer arts and social science graduates. Most political scientists would agree that examining the changing directions of the government's education policy, or any policy, falls within the scope of Political Science. Far fewer, however, would accept the study of internal university politics as subject-matter appropriate for Political Science.

Some students in the International Relations class come from the private sector of education. The existence of private schools is a vigorously contested issue in party politics, but it is sometimes an issue in family politics as well. For some families which want their children educated privately the cost is a considerable burden and a decision is made that only boys will be sent to private schools with girls having to do the best they can in state schools. Is the allocation of scarce resources within the family something of concern to the political scientist? Some, such as Roland Pennock and David Smith, see the family as being well beyond the scope of Political Science. Family decision-making, they argue is quasi-political in nature and cannot be viewed as constituting 'real' politics. To treat the affairs of family life 'as the stuff of politics would do violence to ordinary linguistic usage and would give a distorted view of the family institution, ignoring its generally nonpolitical nature and purposes.'[3] Others disagree with this view and recognise the power structures within the family as being extremely political in nature. Roger King suggests in his chapter that political sociologists would not flinch from examining the family, and Adrian Leftwich has argued that even decisions such as whether to go on holiday or redecorate the kitchen are legitimate topics of political enquiry.[4]

Let us look more closely at the students in the lecture room: why are they there and what is happening to them? Most students enter higher education in order to gain a qualification. Much of what they learn will be forgotten within a few years, perhaps within months. They are studying Political Science as a means of preparing themselves for higher positions in the occupational structure. Universities train the future professional elite and provide them with what Samuel Bowles and Herbert Gintis refer to as the 'skills of domination.'[5] Undergraduates are, then, caught up in a process which leads to continued inequality in society. They will receive higher incomes, have superior working conditions, and even enjoy better health than those whose working lives they will control. This inequality is seen as legitimate by all concerned because those who receive the superior share of life's prizes do so on apparent merit. Should political scientists examine their own professional activity in terms of a process which influences the shape of society? It must be said that many academics exhibit 'ivory tower' tendencies and recognise few if any links between the activity of teaching undergraduates and the nature of the economic and political order which their teaching contributes towards.

Finally what is going on in the International Relations class is reinforcing another related process. The scene is familiar enough with the lecturer providing 'knowledge' and students playing the largely passive role of taking notes. After fifty minutes the lecturer comes to an end and asks if there are any points arising from what has been said which require further clarification. At this point an obliging student might ask a desultory question in order to ease the embarrassment of silence. This quick sketch of events which are repeated time after time reveals aspects of what is sometimes referred to as the 'hidden curriculum' which exists alongside the explicit curriculum of International Relations, and through it students learn 'fitting-in skills' which will prepare them for roles at work and in society. Through the hidden curriculum students learn conformity, deference and to trust the judgments of those in authority. Is this informal political education a legitimate topic for Political Science? Few political scientists would agree that it is.

Students of Political Science will at some stage have to confront the question of what subject-matter is to be included within the scope of the discipline. The brief account above provides examples of topics which might be described as 'political' in nature ranging from the international politics of East and West to the micropolitics of the lecture class. Should Political Science include only the macropolitics of government activity, should it expand so far as to include the micropolitics of the family and classroom, or should the frontier be drawn somewhere between the two? Students will hear and read various arguments put forward as to what constitutes authentic political activity and should therefore be the legitimate concern of the discipline. Evaluating them is likely to be a complex yet rewarding exercise.[6]

POLITICAL THEORY

Exactly what subject-matter constitutes Political Science is, then, a contested issue. There are, however, many political scientists who work within a tradition which has its roots in moral philosophy. They see Political Science primarily in terms of the study of Political Theory. Indeed, many of them are unhappy about the discipline being referred to as 'Political Science' and would prefer another title. In his inaugural lecture Professor Ernest Barker reflected this unease:

> I am not altogether happy about the term 'Science'. It has been vindicated so largely, and almost exclusively, for the exact and experimental study of natural phenomena, that its application to politics may convey suggestions, and excite anticipations, which cannot be justified. If I am to use the designation of Political Science, I shall use it ... to signify a method, a form of enquiry, concerned with the moral phenomena of human behaviour in political studies.[7]

There is some truth in portraying this tradition as being represented by 'armchair theorists' busily making pronouncements about the way things ought to be in society. For, in the first place, traditional political theorists are involved in areas which are heavily normative or prescriptive in nature. In attempting to show the way to a better world, political theorists cannot avoid making value judgments about which political arrangements are better or worse. In the second place, political theorists reflect and speculate on issues rather than go out into the 'real' world and gather information with questionnaires, polls or other measuring devices. This traditional approach will be found throughout the discipline and not just contained within the parts of it labelled Political Theory. For example, John Hertz rejected what he saw as the pseudo-scientific methods of his colleagues engaged in International Relations research who were attempting to quantify various processes. His method lay in a tradition that reached back to ancient Athens and involved no more than the 'application to problems and subject matter at hand of whatever intelligence is available.'[8]

The study of Political Theory can be approached in a number of ways as Alan Lawton explains in his chapter. The most common method involves study of the history of political ideas through examination of the 'great books'. Some political theorists see a tradition within political thought with philosophers criticising and building upon the contributions of their predecessors, and it is this process which leads to the development of logic and progress towards the truth. Although they may have lived at different times, philosophers have been preoccupied in confronting what might be called the perennial questions of politics; 'what is justice?' and 'what is freedom?' but above all 'why should I obey the state?' Alan Lawton examines why the truth in politics remains so elusive. He points out that language is far from being a perfect means of communication, and exploring political ideas becomes complex when the type of society in which they were voiced has long disappeared. The political theorist has to interpret the meaning of actions and statements made by past philosophers in the context of their time before it is possible to understand their significance. Arriving at the truth is constantly blocked by the barriers of time and history.

The tradition of Political Theory suffered a major decline in the years following the Second World War. Political Theory appeared to be threatened by Marxism, although the threat never fully materialised, in which abstract speculation would be replaced by 'scientific' analysis. But the deadliest blow was, as John Horton argued, the awful nightmare of Nazi Germany. He suggested that 'The meaningless death of millions in the extermination camps of one of the most culturally and philosophically sophisticated countries of Europe seemed to leave political philosophy mute and in a condition of hopeless ineffectiveness.'[9] But the events of the late sixties — notably the tragic entanglement of the United States in Vietnam and the social unrest it generated — revived the fortunes of political thought. Today it seems unreasonable to blame Political Theory for the ideas and institutions that led to the terrors of Nazi Germany. At the same time, however, Political Theory must confront the problems that continue to threaten civilization in the latter part of the twentieth century. Political theorists must never again hide from such a challenge.

Alan Lawton recounts how at the time of its low ebb there was a successful hijack of the label 'Political Theory' from the study of the 'great thinkers' to the emerging scientific approaches to the study of politics. In his chapter on International Relations, Steve Smith explores the operation of the new political theories in generating hypotheses and how these hypotheses might be tested directly. Such political theories are not the normative political theories of the philosophers who used logical argument as their method. Champions of the new political theories claimed them to be value-free or ethically-neutral, being neither true nor false but simply more or less 'useful' in explaining the political world.

New political theories tended to fall into one of two broad areas: wide-ranging theories which attempted to explain how the political system functioned, and partial theories which attempted to explain limited phenomena within the political system. New theories of the former type, such as General Systems Theory and Structural-Functionalism, were based on ideas borrowed from other disciplines, notably Biology. They provided an image of the political system as a self-regulating entity in which stability was maintained through constant adaptation to the changing internal and external environments. Although theories such as these, particularly David Easton's systems approach, became a very popular way of looking at political activity their usefulness was limited. For example Michael Goldsmith observes that 'systems theory is not really adequate explanatory theory' in his chapter on Urban Politics. In similar vein, Rod Hague argues that with reference to Comparative Politics the impact of Easton's theory has in fact been illusory. This is because many researchers have paid lip service to the existence of systems theory but because of its highly abstract nature it has not influenced the way in which they proceeded with their research.

An example of the second and more partial type of political theory is contained in Chris Goodrich's chapter on Modern Political Economy. He cites W. Mitchell's claim that the economic approach to the study of politics is the 'shape of political theory to come.' Having borrowed ideas from Public Choice theory, researchers in Modern Political Economy have constructed situations akin to those feared by Hobbes where life was 'solitary, poore, nasty, brutish, and short' and have used gaming techniques to explore how individuals might come together and bargain in order to avoid reverting back to anarchy.

Political Theory is, then, now a rather ambiguous term in Political Science and is one claimed by both philosophical and scientific practitioners.[10] When used in the traditional sense, Political Theory forms one of the twin pillars upon which Political Science is built. It has returned from a period of despair and relative neglect to occupy an important place in the discipline. When used in the sense of 'new' political theory it refers to a way of studying politics which rejects traditional methods as unscientific in nature. The intention was to replace normative theory by empirical theory. To achieve this the new political theorists attempted to emulate the rigorous methods of the natural sciences but this too, as we shall see, resulted in considerable disillusionment.

POLITICAL INSTITUTIONS

The second pillar of Political Science is the institutional tradition in the study of politics. As the name suggests, the institutional approach examines the formal apparatus of government. However the view that political activity is confined solely to within the institutions of government – to within legislatures, executives, judiciaries, political parties, public corporations, local government bureaucracies and the like – has been attacked for presenting a very restricted definition of what politics is. As a result of such criticism the tradition of seeing Political Science as preoccupied with the institutions of government and its agencies suffered a major decline. Professor F. F. Ridley has acknowledged that the field of political institutions has become 'something of an intellectual backwater.'[11] At the same time he restated the traditionalist view and argued that the organised state is an area which the political scientist can truly call his or her own. Even the methods of enquiry can be developed within Political Science and not imported in from outside disciplines. Today the institutional approach is less narrowly conceived than in the past and is enjoying something of a modest revival.

Such a revival is illustrated by the development within Urban Studies, which has largely subsumed the more descriptive and institutionally-based sub-field of Local Government. Because it was built on foundations of constitutional history and law the institutional approach found in Local Government resulted in the structure and legal characteristics of various bodies being described in detail. Researchers within Urban Politics, however, have adopted wider perspectives and are more aware that formal constitutional relations may not correspond with actual negotiated relations that exist between such bodies.

The study of political institutions is represented throughout the discipline. In the pages which follow Rod Hague observes that the institutionally-based Comparative Government tradition is still found within the broader area of Comparative Politics. It takes the form of a 'Cook's Tour' with the most popular destinations being the United States, France and Russia. The approach remains predominantly descriptive, concentrating on the institutions of the state, 'legal and historical in tone.' David Wilson and Neville Woodhead point out that Public Administration focuses a great deal of attention on the institutions of the public sector particularly, but not exclusively, those of central and local government. Within International Relations a study of political institutions is more than incidental when considering issues such as integration theory, international law or the making of foreign policy. For example, it is easy to appreciate that an understanding of British foreign policy demands some knowledge of the organisation, methods and personnel of the Foreign and Commonwealth Office.

Thus the study of political institutions still commands an important place in Political Science encouraged by the fact that the way in which institutions are studied has undergone considerable change. Rather than adopting a narrow approach which focuses on legal and formal structures, contemporary research approaches institutions which evolved gradually amongst political scientists. It was largely the result of a dramatic restructuring of Political Science twenty years ago which is now referred to as the 'behavioural revolution'.

THE AMERICAN IMPACT ON POLITICAL SCIENCE

It has been estimated that over three-quarters of all political scientists work in the United States, and so it should come as no surprise that the development of the discipline has been and remains influenced by American initiatives. Without doubt the most important of such contributions in the postwar years has been the behavioural revolution.[12] This new orientation in Political Science and the other social sciences, behaviouralism, took its name from a branch of psychology founded in the 1930s known as behaviourism. Behaviourists focused their research on gathering observable and measurable psychological data rather than devote resources to grappling with highly abstract notions such as id and ego. In Political Science behaviouralism rejected what up to then had formed the two pillars of the discipline – Political Theory and Political Institutions. It was now argued that since traditional normative theory could not be verified it was 'unscientific' and should be rejected in favour of 'new' theory which could be verified. Behaviouralists also dismissed the study of institutions as being far less important than the study of individual political behaviour. Institutions were seen as merely incidental contexts within which individuals interacted and the process of politics took place.

Behaviouralism is not easy to define precisely, and some have referred to it as being more of a 'mood', 'tendency' or 'movement' within Political Science than a distinct and easily recognisable methodology. One of the main pioneers, David Easton, saw behaviouralism as generating a science of politics modelled after the methodological assumptions of the natural sciences. K. W. Kim has argued that the behavioural approach may be identified by three main characteristics. Firstly, the belief that individuals rather than groups or institutions constitute the proper unit for analysis. Secondly, the demand that facts must be separated from values and, finally, the aspiration that explanations should always run in terms of laws or generalisations and never in terms of descriptive statements about particular occurrences.[13]

In retrospect it is easy to see that some exaggerated and colourful claims were made in the name of behaviouralism. David Easton proclaimed that 'the behavioural approach testifies the coming of age of theory in the social sciences'[14] leaving others to argue that all other methods of inquiry should be discarded since they had little or nothing to offer when compared with the promise held out by behavioural methods. Few political scientists in Britain were impressed by behavioural rhetoric although behaviouralism had considerable impact. In his chapter on Political Methodology, Martin Harrop records that the British response 'was distinctly cooler.' Behaviouralism certainly broadened the perspectives of Political Science but failed to trigger off the fundamental re-evaluation of the discipline that occurred in the United States.

The Critique of Behaviouralism

The new 'scientific' approach to the study of politics did not produce the advances in knowledge that were expected of it initially. Indeed, there was a vigorous attack on behaviouralism not only for failing to deliver the goods once promised but also for the adverse effects it was having on the discipline. Critics complained that behaviouralism was trivialising Political Science; it was not scientific, but it was unduly conservative.

The foundations for the first charge — that of trivialising the discipline — lay in behaviouralists' preference for researching areas where the subject-matter could be measured and quantified. There was the danger that political scientists would ignore the big political issues of the day because they were not suitable for quantification in preference for lesser topics where the scope for using scientific techniques was present. Charles Knight and John Playford, both anti-behavioural in outlook, have argued that many political scientists have become prisoners of their own methodology. They suggested that behaviouralists have to receive positive answers to questions such as 'Is the matter to be examined subject to empirical verification, can it be quantified?'[15] Only then can behaviouralists feel confident enough to proceed with their research. Too often, however, it is with topics of minor significance.

The claim that behaviouralism promoted value-free science in the study of politics also came under close scrutiny. Some countered it by arguing that the behavioural approach contained a hidden conservatism within it. The point was made that behavioural political scientists generally accepted the existing political order as given, researched within it, and did not see it as their role to criticise aspects of society. Accepting the existing political order is, of course, only a short step from expressing a silent preference for the *status quo*; behaviouralism's critics interpreted this as proclaiming a conservative ideology. The same ideology was just under the surface of some of the main theoretical frameworks – notably Structural/Functionalism and Systems Theory – which stressed 'equilibrium' and 'pattern maintenance'. It seemed to some that political forces which 'threatened stability' were too readily labelled as being 'deviant' by behaviouralists. In short, the critics argued that the 'new' political theories were as normative as the old, but unlike the old they masqueraded as 'science'.

Finally the behavioural movement within Political Science became identified with a distrust of popular democracy, as Roger King recounts in his chapter on Political Sociology. Voting studies had revealed that the American electorate was ill-informed about politics and seemed to vote in elections without any rational basis. Behaviouralists became involved in redefining democratic theory so that it matched more closely the reality which they had unearthed. Apathy, once recognised as the antithesis of democracy, was presented as a desirable feature of the political system since it contributed to stability. Behaviouralists who participated in this debate found that they had boxed themselves into a corner relying on arguments which were elitist, conservative and very far from being value-free.

Political Science has passed into what some refer to as the 'post-behavioural' era. It is characterised by more realistic expectations about the nature of the contribution Political Science can make to understanding politics. There is also much greater tolerance for differing approaches and methods, particularly those which are more subjective in nature. But this is not to suggest that Political Science has matured into a long-term stage of stable pluralism. The discipline evolves and changes continually as new generations of political scientists together with the already disaffected challenge and test the orientation of the established.

RECENT DEVELOPMENTS

In his inaugural lecture Ralph Miliband criticised the current condition of Political Science because of its 'excessive empiricism' and 'extreme abstractness' which resulted in students of the discipline emerging without 'much of an idea – or any idea – about the nature of the social order of which the political system is part, its relation to that social order, and the manner in which it serves it – or does not serve it.'[16] He proposed that 'class analysis' would relate study of the political system to wider socio-economic forces and that such an analysis could be best undertaken with the tools of Marxism. Alex Callinicos has echoed Professor Miliband's case against Political Science as currently constructed.[17] He argued that the adoption of Marxist perspectives would enable political scientists to examine the distribution of power in the political system but also to relate this to wider patterns of social and economic inequality. Similar dismay with the current state of the discipline has been expressed in a slightly different context by Anthony Arblaster about his overall conclusion is in line with those above.[18]

Marxism has influenced Political Science but it has never approached becoming the dominant mode of analysis. Neil Casey and Alex Cunliffe recount its influence in Development Studies, and Roger King likewise in Political Sociology – two sub-fields shared with sociology. Neville Woodhead and David Wilson have shown how Marxist concepts have been absorbed by non-Marxist approaches to Political Science which are present in Sociology, a discipline sometimes gently mocked for being 'a dialogue with the ghost of Marx'. Why is Marxism central to Sociology but relatively ignored by political scientists? Part of the answer to this complex question probably lies in the tendency of Marxism to undermine the existence of Political Science as a separate discipline. For Marxists tend to see political phenomena as mere manifestations of social and economic forces. It is, therefore, understandable that political scientists defend their discipline and resist moves to have it subsumed and diminished within a wider study of society.

There has also been a recent debate on 'redefining' the scope of Political Science. Adrian Leftwich has argued that the Western view of what constitutes political activity blinkers out the study of phenomena which are essentially political in nature.[19] His argument is that politics is central to the life of the human species, and that this is an activity which is universal in scope and not confined to the formal institutions of government. He has illuminated this with an examination of societies such as the hunting and gathering Kung San of the Kalahari and the pastoral Maasai of East Africa. What is revealed is that traditional Western definitions of 'politics' portrays such societies as being 'simple' or 'primitive'. A wider definition, however, reveals them as having developed highly sophisticated means for organising the culture and relations which precondition the occurrence of political activity.

Over twenty years ago Chadwick Alger was arguing something similar within the context of the time. He felt that future development of International Relations could benefit from an open-minded exploration of such societies since 'primitive societies seem not to be as simple, in terms vital to the social scientist, as has been presumed.'[20] In more recent times Robert Dowse has speculated on ways in which Political Sociology might be rejuvenated and provided with a new intellectual focus.[21] His proposal involved revisiting the same sort of society as Adrian Leftwich with a view to studying kinship systems and the ways in which such systems coped with threats to their survival. It may also be possible that redefinitions – be they novel in scope or focus – will occur in areas which have previously been neglected. Graham Smith has portrayed Political Geography as the Cinderella of the discipline despite long repeated calls that it 'should become an established field of Political Science.'[22] It is true that the spatial dimension has become an important consideration in many sub-fields of Political Science but nevertheless the sizable contribution that Human Geography could make remains largely unexploited. Or, rather than relaunching an existing area redefinitions might develop from emerging issues such as multiculturalism and feminism.

It is unlikely that the debate about the nature of Political Science will end in a definite or widely-accepted conclusion. In some ways the very structure of the discipline ensures that the identity of the discipline remains a contested issue. The accounts below reflect the state of flux that is found across the discipline: ' . . . there is little consensus about the present nature of Comparative Politics' . . . 'political sociologists have constantly bewailed what they regard as the subject's fragmentation and lack of focus' . . . 'the subject matter of Urban Politics has changed considerably in scope and emphasis in recent years' . . . 'one of the major problems in the study of International Relations has been, and remains, that of deciding what its subject-area is.' Lack of certainty could be diagnosed, rather pessimistically, as the torments of a declining discipline in search of the focus and direction that it once

14

possessed. Alternatively, it may be interpreted as the condition of any discipline which resists the lure of comfortable fossilisation in preference for new challenges and subsequent intellectual development.

● NOTES

1. See, for example, the surveys conducted by Stephen Tansey, 'Politics courses in higher education: an overview', Teaching Politics, Volume 10 (1981), 13-26; 'Politics courses in higher education: review of recent developments', Teaching Politics, Volume 11 (1982), 259-277; 'Politics courses in higher education: developments in 1982/3', Teaching Politics, Volume 12 (1983), 291-299.

2. Adrian Leftwich (ed.): What is Politics (Oxford: Basil Blackwell, 1984) 6.

3. J. Roland Pennock and David G. Smith: Political Science (New York: Collier-Macmillan, 1964) 6.

4. Adrian Leftwich: Redefining Politics (London: Methuen, 1983) 22.

5. Samuel Bowles and Herbert Gintis: Schooling in Capitalist America (London: Routledge and Kegan Paul, 1976) 12.

6. See Peter Nicholson, 'What is Politics: determining the scope of Political Science', Politico, Volume XL11 (1977) 228-249.

7. E. Barker, 'The study of Political Science' in Preston King (ed.): The Study of Politics: a collection of inaugural lectures (London: Frank Cass, 1977) 17-34.

8. J. H. Hertz: International Politics in the Atomic Age (New York: Columbia University Press, 1962) v.

9. John Horton, 'Political philosophy and politics' in Adrian Leftwich (ed.): What is Politics? (Oxford: Basil Blackwell, 1984) 115.

10. See John S. Nelson (ed.): What Should Political Theory be Now? (Albany: State University of New York Press, 1983).

11. F. F. Ridley: The Study of Government: Political Science and Public Administration (London: George Allen and Unwin, 1975) 25.

12. For a wider discussion of the American contribution see Bernard Crick: The American Science of Politics (London: Routledge and Kegan Paul, 1959) and for a discussion of behaviouralism in Political Science see Dennis Kavanagh: Political Science and Political Behaviour (London: George Allen and Unwin, 1983).

13. K. W. Kim, 'The limits of behavioral explanation in politics' in Charles A. McCoy and John Playford (eds.): Apolitical Politics: a critique of behavioralism (New York: Thomas Y. Crowell, 1967) 38-54.

14. David Easton: A Framework for Political Analysis (Englewood Cliffs, N.J.: Prentice-Hall, 1965) 22.

15. McCoy and Playford, op. cit., 7.

16. Ralph Miliband, 'Teaching politics in an age of crisis', Times Higher Educational Supplement (19.3.76).

17. Alex Callinicos, 'Marxism and Politics' in Adrian Leftwich (ed.): What is Politics? (Oxford: Basil Blackwell, 1984) 125.

18. See Anthony Arblaster, 'Developments in the study of politics: tradition, 'science' and Marxism' in Barry Dufour (ed.): New Movements in the Social Sciences and Humanities (London: Maurice Temple Smith, 1982) 49-63.

19. Adrian Leftwich: Redefining Politics (London: Methuen, 1983).

20. Chadwick F. Alger, 'Comparison of intranational and international politics' in R. Barry Farrell (ed.): Approaches to Comparative and International Politics (Evanston: Northwestern University Press, 1966) 301-328. The article was originally published in the American Political Science Review, Volume LV11 (1963) 406-19.

21. Robert E. Dowse, 'Political Sociology: a modest proposal', Teaching Politics, Volume 12 (1983) 18-26.

22. See, for example, Harold H. Sprout, 'Political Geography as a Political Science field', American Political Science Review, Volume XXV (1931) 439-442.

SELECT BIBLIOGRAPHY

Jean Blondel: The Discipline of Politics (London: Butterworths, 1981).

Adrian Leftwich: Redefining Politics (London: Methuen, 1983).

Adrian Leftwich (ed.): What is Politics? (Oxford: Basil Blackwell, 1984).

Geoffrey Pontin & Peter Gill: Introduction to Politics (Oxford: Martin Robertson, 1982).

Political Theory

Alan Lawton

Recent discussions within Political Theory have assumed that the subject is once again 'alive and kicking' after its 'death' was announced in the early 1950s. There is now a wealth of literature concerned with Political Theory which suggests that either the death was prematurely diagnosed or that the wrong corpse was, in fact, identified. This state of affairs arose partly because of the confusion over what exactly Political Theory was and what it was supposed to do. In this paper I shall examine various ways of considering Political Theory and offer notice of recent discussions within the field from the perspectives of history and philosophy.

POLITICAL THEORY AND HISTORY

A common approach to Political Theory is that of offering the reader a general survey of the history of political ideas of Western theorists in a more or less straightforward chronological sequence. Sabine's *History of Political Theory* is characteristic of this approach where the history of political ideas is traced from the early Greeks, through Medieval Scholasticism, to the works of Hobbes, Locke, Mill and so on. From this perspective the concern may be to express the notion that political ideas exist over time and we can trace the history of their usage. This approach is often characterised as a particular tradition of writing about politics so that if we wish to examine concepts such as 'justice' we can look at the way in which the concept has been used by various theorists in the hope that past usage can illuminate our present discussion of politics. Studies in the history of ideas are conceived of as having direct relevance to contemporary problems.

Sabine assumes that there is a distinct tradition of Political Theory comprising the classic texts of political literature and that this tradition indicates the framework within which particular works should be interpreted. S. Wolin in *Politics and Vision* considers the idea of a tradition of discourse about political ideas as a 'Grand Dialogue' where an understanding of the tradition is essential for an understanding of contemporary politics. Central to Wolin's argument about the tradition is the thesis that:

> ... most formal political speculation has operated simultaneously at *two* different levels. At one level every political philosopher has concerned himself with what he thinks to be a vital problem of his day. At another level, however, ... many political writings ... have been meant as a contribution to the continuing dialogue of Western political philosophy.[1]

For Wolin there are thus two different levels of intention that must be examined when interpreting a particular work and the principal one involves the author's concern to participate in the tradition. To understand, say, Locke we must, therefore, take into account his intention to refute Hobbes. There is a sense in which, for Wolin, the theorist enters into a debate, or a dialogue, where the terms of reference have already been set out and he becomes a participant in the tradition of political thought that forms an inherited body of knowledge bringing together past and present political experience.

What is apparent with such an approach is the consensus on such matters as the historical reality of the tradition with an identification of its major participants and their role in the development of the tradition. Thus the works of Plato, Aristotle, Aquinas, Machiavelli, Hobbes, Locke and J. S. Mill are examined but not those of Spinoza or Heidegger.

For J. G. Gunnell,[2] however, the idea of *the* tradition is not so much a research conclusion as an *a priori* construct. It has come to inform the interpretation of particular works both in that they are viewed as elements of a tradition and that a meaning is attributed to them which is derived from a particular conception of the tradition as a whole. From various perspectives such concepts as 'obligation', 'justice', 'authority' or 'freedom' are discussed but this may well be 'merely a matter of imposing analytical categories and of describing them from a particular standpoint.'[3] Gunnell considers that the authors of the classic works in Political Theory did see themselves as addressing issues of timeless and universal significance, and that occasionally a similarity, or a continuity, existed in the discussion of certain problems and was recognised as such by the theorists themselves. There are instances, Gunnell suggests, when a theorist noted a similarity between his enterprise and that of a predecessor; or occasions when an author has explic-

itly directed arguments towards a past thinker; or even historical connections between the works of one author and their influence on another,
e.g. the influence on Aquinas of the political thought of Aristotle.
Despite connections such as these which may well be relevant in the
interpretation of certain specific texts, Gunnell argues that they also
may be quite insignificant and become exaggerated if we assume that
the theorist's main concern is to participate in the 'Great Dialogue'.
In any event, although such connections may lend force to the idea of
the tradition, they in no way give substance either to the assumption of
the tradition or to the claims about it:

> It may well be that individual texts may very well be part of some trad-
> ition in philosophy or other form of thought and participate in it, con-
> sciously or unconsciously, but this in no way substantiates the idea of
> *the* tradition.[4]

Gunnell's basic theme is that certain of the classic works are instances
of a 'creative mind's encounter' with the problems of political order.
Such works may possess certain similarities and 'family resemblances'
and possess certain common features but this does not necessarily entail
the idea of the tradition.

In the early 1950s the political scientists who championed the cause
of behavioural politics, (the idea of a science of politics modelled after
the methodology of the natural sciences) were intent on establishing
the autonomy of Political Theory as an empirical science and rescuing
Political Theory from an identification with the history of ideas and its
concern with the study of the classic texts from Plato onwards. David
Easton,[5] diagnosing the 'impoverishment' of Political Theory, argued
that traditional Political Theory as practised by Plato, Aristotle *et al.*
had given way to the history of ideas and as such had been reduced to
a form of historical analysis that 'lived parasitically on the ideas of the
past'. Easton considered that Political Theory had relinquished its
traditional role of building a systematic theory about political conduct
and political institutions and was no longer concerned to construct a
normative frame of reference. Although Easton was concerned to
emphasise the need for a revival of normative theory, his principal
aim was to distinguish discussions of values from descriptions and
explanations of facts and to further the development of a purely empirical science of politics.

Although individuals such as Quentin Skinner[6] argue that it is probably impossible for an interpreter of a work to attain complete object-

ivity by eliminating all preconceptions, Skinner maintains that the first goal of historical investigation must be to understand the meaning of a text through a recovery of the author's intentions. This requires, insofar as possible, a neutralisation of the influence of the interpreter's own values. Drawing examples from various works dealing with the history of political ideas, Skinner catalogues the range of fallacies in interpretation that, in his view, arise from a failure to recognise that the recovery of the meaning of texts 'presupposes the grasp both of what they were intended to mean, and how this meaning was intended to be taken.'[7] Skinner considers that much of the work in the history of ideas has involved the unwarranted impositions of modern assumptions and categories of analysis on the text; the extremes of either seeking the author's meaning from an analysis of the text alone or attempting to view this meaning simply as an expression of a particular social context; a failure to distinguish an explanation of a work from an understanding of what the author was saying.

The work of Skinner is characteristic of a developing interest in the methodological problems involved in the interpretation of the classical texts and reflects a growing concern about the nature of understanding and explanation within the social sciences generally. In order to understand a text Skinner suggests that we must acknowledge the 'special authority of an agent over his intentions'[8] and we uncover the author's intentions by taking account of the general context within which a text was written. We begin the task, not by making an intensive study of the text itself, but rather by trying to see what relations it bears to existing conventions be they moral, political, social or otherwise. By way of example, Skinner suggests that Machiavelli's *The Prince* was, in part, intended as a deliberate attack on the moral conventions of advicebooks to princes and this is not a fact contained in the text itself.[9]

Skinner is not alone in suggesting that much of the work in the history of ideas suffers from methodological deficiencies and his debt to the work of John Dunn is explicitly acknowledged. Dunn[10] emphasises the unhistorical character of many of the studies in the history of ideas contending that such histories have often been histories of abstractions and fictions 'conjured' up in the present and read back into the past. This does not constitute, for Dunn, an historical account of something actually existing in the past.

Both Skinner and Dunn are concerned to suggest that social action must be understood in terms of its meaning for the actor and that this meaning can be ascertained by viewing the action as part of a context of the rules and conventions of social activity. The intention is to confront the problem of historicism, or the problem of how the interpreter can transcend the influence of his own subjectivity and historical circumstances and gain an adequate understanding of the past and the actual meaning of historical texts rather than merely assess their significance from the perspective of the present.

POLITICAL THEORY AND PHILOSOPHY

The second approach to Political Theory to be examined is one which has reflected developments within the field of philosophy. Initial impetus was given by the work of A. J. Ayer[11] who suggested that there are only two kinds of meaningful propositions: those which are analytically true and those which are factually true. From the first perspective the concern is with the logical structure of arguments and their internal coherence so that their truth or falsity is determined by internal logic. In contrast, the truth or falsity of the second perspective is dependent upon correspondence with an external reality. Thus the sort of statements that we find in traditional Political Theory, e.g. 'The state should seek the good for its members', are neither true by definition nor by verification with the implication that all statements of value, all recommendations and prescriptions are denied meaning.

Much of traditional Political Theory is unphilosophical since the proper business of philosophy is seen as clarification and analysis. Taking this view, philosophy is seen, essentially, as a second-order activity within which it is not the job of the philosopher to describe or explain the world. His task is to clarify or analyse the concepts, the arguments, assumptions and methods of the first-order activities.

T. D. Weldon's *The Vocabulary of Politics* was heavily influenced by the work of logical positivists such as Ayer. Weldon offers a radical critique of the conventional content of traditional Political Theory:

> The greater part of classical political philosophy really is concerned with recommending and providing worthless logical grounds for the adoption or perpetuation of axioms and definitions involving political words like 'state', 'law' and 'rights'.[12]

Weldon believed that the task of philosophy was to merely sort out linguistic muddles and he suggests that words like 'state', 'citizen', etc., do not have intrinsic or essential meanings to be discovered and explained by political theorists. The fallacy of 'essentialism' has led to the raising of spurious problems from a failure to understand the logic of language.

From this perspective it is considered misleading to ask such questions as 'Why am I obligated to obey the state?' Belonging to society involves the acceptance of *rules* and our concept of promises, contracts and obligations are learnt and not chosen in a vacuum so that understanding what it is to be social would be impossible unless we understand what it is to have rights and obligations and vice versa. Having obligations is inseparable from living in society; that we have obligations is, therefore, not an empirical fact which calls for explanation or justification, but is an analytic proposition. Thus claims such as 'A has an obligation to do x' are to be considered as claims to the effect that 'A's case falls under a social rule directing people in such circumstances to do x', and any *general* question of the form 'Why should we accept obligations?' is misconceived since having obligations is part of what living in society means. 'Living in society' is treated as being synonymous with the concept of citizenship and 'Why am I obligated to the state?' is seen as a meaningless question since ' ... to call something the government is precisely to imply that it ought to be obeyed.'[13]

The central questions of traditional Political Theory are seen as nonsensical from the point of view of the linguistic analyst. Questions such as 'Is liberty a good thing?', 'What is the true nature of justice?', or 'Is democracy the ideal form of polity?' are seen as either too general or betraying a mistaken essentialism. Words simply have uses and if we wish to examine the variety of uses to which a concept may be put it is necessary, at the outset, to establish the range and limits of the concept's use. Thus Berlin[14] examines two concepts of liberty; Miller[15] distinguishes three concepts of social justice; and Schumpeter[16] isolates two concepts of democracy.

Critics of the method of linguistic analysis suggest that it has only a limited use in helping us to understand political ideas. Miller[17] suggests that the linguistic analyst runs the risk of 'temporary parochialism' in that he examines the way in which his contemporaries use certain concepts and loses sight of the historical changes to which those concepts have been subject. Instead of clarifying the use of a concept such as 'liberty' it may well be that the linguistic analyst has clarified the meaning for the members of a particular society at a given time. Not only does this offer us an incomplete account of the meaning of a term, but it also carries the further risk that concepts currently undergoing a change of meaning will be ossified by the analyst's method so that he will either overlook the change altogether or else actively intervene on the side of linguistic conservatism by describing the new applications of a particular concept as misuses. The fact that political concepts change their meaning over time limits the usefulness of the linguistic method in understanding them.

A second line of criticism is that of C. Pateman[18] who suggests that arguments about the general nature of political obligation and the relationship of the individual and the state have been used to justify specific political institutions where political obligation is seen as un-problematical anyway; McPherson, for example, writes that his arguments are intended to apply to the 'liberal-democratic state'.[19]

Given these criticisms, the work of the linguistic analyst is now considered to be the starting point for Political Theory but not the whole of it. Developments within the philosophy of the social sciences have suggested that the doctrine that all genuine statements must be analytic or empirical is not, in fact, true. C. Taylor[20] has explicitly attacked the view that questions of value are independent of questions of fact, arguing instead that a given framework of explanation tends to support an associated value position so that insofar as Political Theory cannot do without an explanatory framework it cannot stop producing normative theory. What is believed to be true in a particular society at a given time can be shown to be the product of certain historical factors at work in that society. Marx, for example, treated prescriptive Political Theory as reflections of prevailing socio-economic conditions and of the positions of their authors under those conditions. While political theorists might speak in universal terms, their doctrines express the interests of some class or group in society.

It was noted in the Introduction to the fourth series of *Philosophy, Politics and Society*[21] that an increasing awareness of ideology had helped Political Theory escape from the hubris that brought about its 'death'. Rawls' *A Theory of Justice* is just one work that represents a return to Political Theory in the grand manner, i.e. it is an attempt to derive notions of 'justice' on the basis of presuppositions about man's basic nature and values. It rejects the idea that normative analysis is taboo and the notion that political philosophy is no more than a hand-maiden to other disciplines. Downie[22] posits the view that, although Political Theory will properly concentrate on the concepts, principles and presuppositions of political life, in order to complete its task it will connect these with a theory of human nature. This, Downie suggests, is the appeal of Plato, Aristotle, Hobbes *et al.* in that they all provide a total vision of man and society, and these visions are intellectually satisfying.

CONCLUSION

The different strands that emerge from this brief discussion of recent trends in Political Theory indicate that the subject has been revitalised since its demise was heralded in the early 1950s. At one level there has been an increasing concern with problems within the methodology of the social sciences in general coupled with a preoccupation with problems within the philosophy of history. The concern is to elucidate the intentions of political theorists by examining the historical context of the classic works of Political Theory. At another level, concern with the fact-value distinction has re-established the place of normative theory so that one of the objects of Political Theory is considered to be helping us to decide what political ends we should pursue and how we should go about pursuing them. The rejection of the positivist framework has meant the rejection of linguistic analysis in a narrow sense; it is deemed necessary to examine a concept's place within the whole set of beliefs and values that constitute social life. Following on from this, a concern with the problem of ideology has become a central theme in Political Theory. Finally, a concern with certain perennial questions such as the nature of the state, its origins, form of and justification of, has been replaced, to some extent, with a concern with concepts and principles specifying the ends of government. Characteristically this has taken the form of discussions about liberty, equality, rights or justice in terms of which government policies can be evaluated. The current literature of Political Theory offers a rich diversity in the various themes outlined above.

● NOTES

1. S. Wolin: Politics and Vision (Boston: Little, Brown, 1960), 25.

2. J. G. Gunnell: Political Theory: Tradition and Interpretation (Cambridge Mass.: Winthrop Publishers Inc., 1979).

24

3. Ibid., 85.

4. Ibid., 88.

5. D. Easton, 'Decline of Modern Political Theory', Journal of Politics Volume 13 (1951).

6. Q. Skinner, 'Meaning and Understanding in the History of Ideas', History and Theory, Volume 8 (1969).

7. Ibid., 48.

8. Ibid., 48.

9. Q. Skinner, 'Social Meaning and the Explanation of Social Action' in P. Laslett, W. G. Runciman & Q. Skinner: Philosophy, Politics and Society. Fourth Series (Oxford: Basil Blackwell, 1972).

10. J. Dunn, 'The Identity of the History of Ideas' in P. Laslett, W. G. Runciman & Q. Skinner: Philosophy, Politics and Society. Fourth Series (Oxford: Basil Blackwell, 1972).

11. A. J. Ayer: Language, Truth and Logic (2nd ed.), (Harmondsworth: Penguin, 1971).

12. T. D. Weldon: The Vocabulary of Politics (Penguin, 1953), 41.

13. T. McPherson: Political Obligation (Routledge and Kegan Paul, 1967), 59.

14. I. Berlin, 'Two Concepts of Liberty' in Four Essays on Liberty (Oxford: Clarendon Press 1969).

15. D. Miller: Social Justice (Oxford: Clarendon Press, 1976).

16. J. Schumpeter: Capitalism, Socialism and Democracy (London: Allen & Unwin, 1954).

17. Miller, op. cit., 3.

18. C. Pateman, 'Political Obligation and Conceptual Analysis', Political Studies (1973).

19. McPherson, op. cit.

20. C. Taylor, 'Neutrality in Political Science' in P. Laslett & W. G. Runciman (eds.): Philosophy, Politics and Society. Third Series (Oxford: Basil Blackwell, 1967).

21. P. Laslett, W. G. Runciman & Q. Skinner (eds.): Philosophy, Politics and Society. Fourth Series (Oxford: Basil Blackwell, 1972).

22. R. S. Downie, 'Analogies and Relevance in Political Philosophy', Political Studies (1973).

SELECT BIBLIOGRAPHY

B. Barry: Political Argument (London: Routledge and Kegan Paul, 1965).

R. G. Collingwood: The Idea of History (Oxford: Clarendon Press, 1946).

A. de Crespigny and A. Wertheimer (eds.): Contemporary Political Theory (London: Thomas Nelson and Sons Ltd., 1970).

R. E. Flathman: Concepts in Social and Political Philosophy (London: Macmillan, 1973). The Practice of Rights (Cambridge: Cambridge University Press, 1976).

H. L. A. Hart: The Concept of Law (Oxford: Oxford University Press, 1961).

V. Held (ed.): Philosophy and Political Action (London: Oxford University Press, 1972).

S. Lukes: Power: A Radical View (London: Macmillan, 1974).

A. Macintyre: Against the Self-Images of the Age: Essays on Ideology and Philosophy (London: Duckworth, 1971).

D. J. Manning: Liberalism (London: J. M. Dent and Sons Ltd., 1976).

M. Oakeshott: Rationalism in Politics (London: Methuen and Co., 1962).

P. P. Nicholson, 'Political Theory and Political Practice' in Political Studies, Volume XXI, 1973.

C. Pateman: The Problem of Political Obligation (Chichester: J. Wiley, 1979).

J. G. A. Pocock: Politics, Language and Time (New York: Atheneum, 1971).

A. Quinton (ed.): Political Philosophy (Oxford: Oxford University Press, 1967).

D. D. Raphael: Problems of Political Philosophy (London: Pall Mall, 1970).

J. C. Rees: Equality (London: Macmillan, 1972).

A. Ryan: Philosophy of the Social Sciences (London: Macmillan, 1970).

J. Searle: Speech Acts (Cambridge: Cambridge University Press, 1969).

C. Taylor, 'Interpretation and the Sciences of Man' in Review of Metaphysics, 1971.

P. Winch: The Idea of a Social Science and its Relation to Philosophy (London: Routledge and Kegan Paul, 1958).

B. Williams, 'The Idea of Equality' in P. Laslett and W. G. Runciman (eds.) Philosophy, Politics and Society, Second Series (Oxford: Basil Blackwell, 1962).

Comparative Politics

Rod Hague

When we begin to study government with curiosity, at the same instant we
begin to compare: the problem is not whether to compare but how to
organise comparison.

(W. J. M. Mackenzie, *Politics and Social Science* (Harmondsworth:
Penguin, 1967) 311)

What is comparison and why should we study politics in a comparative way? To compare is to estimate the extent of similarity or difference between one thing and another. We compare because we can do
no other: 'Margaret Thatcher is the most dominant prime minister
since Churchill'; 'Reagan has been more successful than Carter in
handling Congress'; 'The Soviet Union has become less repressive since
Stalin's time.' Comparison is an inherent methodological assumption,
implicit or overt in the very categories through which we study
politics.[1] In a sense, to speak of *comparative* politics is redundant.
Nonetheless, it is conventionally accorded its own niche within Political
Science; students take courses in it, researchers specialise in it. In what?
It is not easy to find a snappy way to distinguish Comparative Politics
from the rest of Political Science. As Salamon has commented (*à
propos* comparative history), like the elephant in the old story, the
beast seems to be different depending on who touches it and where.[2]

DEFINING COMPARATIVE POLITICS

The difference between Comparative Politics and other areas might be
located in any of three ways: its method, its field or its purpose.
Firstly, Comparative Politics could be characterised as using rigorous
and explicit comparison by contrast with research which is essentially
monographic, emphasising description, particular circumstance and the
singular event. Comparison is not absent from monographic accounts
but plays a latent or subordinate role within them. Comparative and
monographic approaches complement rather than conflict with one
another, but they thrust in different directions: the comparative
towards generalisation, the monographic towards particularity.

Comparative method is not the preserve of Comparative Politics within the wider ambit of Political Science. But comparison should perhaps be methodically done to qualify as 'comparative' Politics, specifying precisely what is to be compared, why and how. This necessitates a careful definition of the research problem, the focus of enquiry within it, the selection of cases appropriate to it and the forms of comparison to be made. This tells us nothing, however, about the content of the subject.

In the second place, Comparative Politics could perhaps be identified as a particular field within the academic study of politics: the study of foreign governments. Such a perspective is epitomised by the traditional 'Cook's Tour' country-by-country course, visiting America, France and Russia in turn (the home country — whichever it happens to be — usually defined out of the course as not being 'foreign'). At one time, this was probably a valid characterisation when the state was the only recognised focus for comparative enquiry. Comparative *Government* was the study of nation-state governments, concentrating on the analysis of constitutions and the other formal structures of government. This approach lost ground in favour of a more inclusive notion of Comparative *Politics* with wider connotations. Frequently, if not invariably, the latter employs the idea of the political system, rather than the state, as an organising metaphor. As a summary definition, Comparative Politics might be said to encompass comparisons between and within political systems. The problem with such a definition is that it renders the field of Comparative Politics even less distinctive, since comparison *within* systems falls under its scope (for instance, an analysis of regional variations in electoral support in Britain, or a comparison of the party system in France under the Fourth and the Fifth Republics). There is a case for limiting the scope of Comparative Politics to comparisons between two or more systems, i.e. to cross-national comparison. But to do so would be essentially stipulative, excluding a great deal that at present purports to be within its scope. It would exclude all single-country studies, for instance. Though not cross-national, such studies may be comparative in method: Rigby has analysed the changing composition and sources of recruitment to the Soviet Communist Party for different periods;[3] Mayhew compared the impact of party, constituency and interest group pressures upon members of Congress.[4] Careful and accurate single-country studies are likely to be a pre-requisite, on most occasions, for useful cross-national comparison. The two are complementary. A further problem with defining Comparative Politics in terms either of cross-national or cross-system comparison is that, although 'nation-state' and 'political system' are often treated as near synonyms, they are not identical categories. As we shall see, neither is immune from difficulties if proposed as *the* standard unit for comparison. What they do have in common, one might comment, is a convenient theoretical fuzziness.

A third way in which Comparative Politics might be characterised is in terms of the aspirations of those engaged in it. As Roy Macridis declared, the function of comparative study is to identify uniformities and differences and to explain them.[5] One can portray Comparative Politics as having been in part an academic movement, centred around certain leading practitioners (or gurus if you prefer), who subscribed to a positivist vision of Political Science.[6] That is, their eventual aim was to develop a global science of politics comprising law-like generalisations, along the lines of the 'hard' laboratory-based sciences like physics or chemistry. Such a science of politics would be inescapably comparative, embracing as it would all societies, at every level from the micro-politics of the individual to the macro-politics of world organisations like the United Nations. The positivist does not doubt that the road ahead is strewn with obstacles, but with the infectious (or is it infuriating?) cheerfulness of Pollyanna, insists that the goal can be reached. Comparative method is, for the travellers on this journey, their handmaiden: an indispensable substitute for the controlled methods of laboratory experimentation largely denied to the social scientist. We will argue that faith in this positivist project has been dimmed, though not extinguished, in recent years. In particular, the notion of a 'meta-theory', integrating all findings beneath a single theoretical umbrella, has become distinctly unfashionable within mainstream academic Political Science.

If this excursion into definition reveals anything, it is that there is little consensus about the present nature of Comparative Politics — except that it lacks consensus. The range of themes and issues encountered in the research literature is extremely diverse and hard to portray overall. Three things might be said. For all its attendant problems, cross-national comparison is the archetype of comparative research, because of the importance that most political scientists, rightly or wrongly, attach to the nation-state. Secondly, the impulse of comparison is towards generalisation, even though single-country studies predominate numerically, even in the main professional outlets for Comparative Politics (the old tradition of foreign political studies masquerading under the comparative label, one might say.)[7] Thirdly, despite the present lack of enthusiasm for global theory, we shall argue there are indications that research in particular areas of Comparative Politics is beginning to knit together.

SOME PROBLEMS OF COMPARISON

Comparison begins with a puzzle or question: 'Do parties in office carry out election pledges?' 'Is inequality growing or declining within Communist systems?' 'Why do some countries seem more prone than others to military seizures of power?' A simple sketch of the research process depicts a tentative explanation, or theory, being put forward and tested, by applying it to one or more cases. As theories are progressively modified in the light of previous research and re-tested, so understanding grows. Research is both iterative and cumulative. Promising theories are confirmed, bad ones discarded. In practice things are not as tidy as this. The political scientist is confronted with numerous variables, which are almost all hard to isolate or to quantify. Cases come ready-made: they are not constructed experimentally in the laboratory. The factors in one case, so far as they can be ascertained, have to be compared with those present (or absent) in another. But which facts and factors are most relevant? Comparative research involves a set of interrelated choices in which theory and problem interact.[8] What is to be compared and how depends on the theorising which guides the investigation, but this in turn must take account of the operational difficulties presented by the research problem and the data available. A crucial skill in the research process is to ask the right questions. That is, to frame questions in such a way that definite answers emerge, whether these confirm the initial theory or disprove it. A theory which cannot be tested because evidence is unavailable, unsuitable or unusable remains mere speculation.

Once the research problem has been initially formulated, the strategy of comparison can be worked out. The main dimensions of choice have been usefully summarised by Roberts:

> [The] problem of strategy involves three dimensions of decision: the *unit* of comparison which may be the political system itself, as a relatively autonomous structure – for example the state, or a sub-system unit, such as a province, a political party or a trade union; the *level* of comparison, which may be intra-system such as local authorities in Britain or cross-system, and the *temporal* context, which may be simultaneous

(comparison of units at some common moment or period) or 'historical' (comparison across different periods or at dissimilar moments of time.)[9]

The strategy adopted also involves the selection of cases, because different approaches are possible. Since comparison is the political scientist's main substitute for controlled experimentation, one way of approximating to laboratory conditions is to pursue a 'most similar' technique. That is, to select cases for comparison that are as closely matched as possible. The researcher is better able to isolate the variables of interest, with some assurance that the effect of background factors is relatively constant. This approach has been used, for instance to investigate in a precise way the relationships between party competition, socio-economic development and welfare levels among the different states of the USA.[10] The 'most similar' technique seems suitable where cases 'bounded' by geography, language, culture or other attributes can be used as the units of comparison. It might, for instance, be fruitfully employed in a comparative study of the Scandinavian political systems, or of the Anglo-Saxon parliamentary democracies in which similar legal, cultural and political norms prevail. The limitations of the approach are that the range of variation in the factors that interest the researcher is likely to be modest, and such differences are in any event likely to be 'over-determined' by numerous entangled factors. Moreover, one cannot be sure how far the resultant findings would apply outside the context in which they were studied.[11]

Often, however, a 'most similar' approach is not feasible. Someone studying, say, the causes of revolution is confronted by relatively few cases, each involving a morass of contributory factors and widely dispersed in time and place. It is possible to make a virtue of necessity. The 'most different' technique involves examining widely dissimilar cases to see what, if anything, they have in common. In a celebrated study, Crane Brinton considered the English, American, French and Russian revolutions, in an effort to discern whether any conditions were present in all cases. He concluded that there were, among them institutional blockage, alienation of the intellectuals, loss of self-confidence among the ruling class, and increased social antagonisms.[12] Subsequent writers have extended the range of cases and the scope of explanation, modifying Brinton's argument about the causes of revolution in the process. But the point is that the examination of widely divergent cases can still contribute to our understanding of the phenomenon of revolution itself, providing that the concept itself does not become hopelessly 'stretched' in the process.

As the quotation from Roberts indicated, time is an important dimension of comparative analysis. Many comparisons are (relatively) simultaneous. The policy styles of West European governments in the 1980s is the focus of one recent study.[13] In practice, such studies often need to be extended backwards in time, to ascertain whether or not the findings are an artefact of the moment. Thus, budgetary comparisons between nations — or local authorities — would be more reliable if they extended over several years. Anthony King studied differences in the policies pursued by governments in five western countries in the early 1970s, considering a range of possible explanations for the patterns encountered.[14] He concluded that the differences between the United States and the other countries were mainly attributable to the different ideas held by US politicians. How the patterns have emerged required a considerable amount of historical discussion. The time-dimension may be a striking feature of some comparative research, though it presents equally striking difficulties of evidence, definition and interpretation. S. N. Eisenstadt's work on the bureaucratic empires ranges across centuries as well as continents, from Ancient Egypt and China, Imperial Rome to the Incas of Peru.[15] Other notable ventures into comparative history have included Barrington Moore's massive study of different pathways to modernity and, stimulated by it, Skocpol's analysis of the French, Russian and Chinese revolutions.[16] The work of Lipset and Rokkan, among others, on the historical stages in the development of party systems in Western Europe has been a highly fertile source of ideas for other scholars.[17]

Most of the examples so far cited involve cross-national comparison. The 150 or so nation-states of the world are of particular interest to political scientists, because they claim sovereign authority, both over their populations and with regard to other states. Statehood and nationhood are both, in fact, matters of degree and some so-called nation-states seem far from being either. Even among the nation-states with undisputed credentials, interdependence rather than independence is the norm. Sovereignty is a fiction, but an important one which affects and can reshape the pattern of political, economic and social relationships within and between societies. This is the basic reason for studying governments. They are important.

But why compare nation-states? Because comparison enlarges the range of cases available to us, and combats enthnocentrism. First Montaigne and then Pascal observed, 'Truth on this side of the Pyrenees, error on the other.'[18] We compare in order to escape from ethnocentric assumptions: that what applies here obtains elsewhere or that the British way of politics – or the American or whatever – is simply best. In other words, cross-national comparison helps to reduce the distorting effects of culture bias upon our understanding of politics. A second reason is that comparison tests the validity of explanations more effectively than studies based only on single countries. Duverger formed his conclusions about the effects of electoral law upon the party system (that first-past-the-post favours a two-party system, while proportional representation produces multi-partyism) upon the evidence of a handful of countries.[19] Rae took the same problem and studied the effects of electoral technique in 23 liberal democracies. His findings, overall, broadly confirmed those of Duverger but were more systematically based.[20]

There are, of course, numerous problems with cross-national comparison. Although as Betrand de Jouvenel commented, some scholars believe they can derive everything from GNP statistics, information is often patchy, untrustworthy or simply unobtainable for many societies. Reliable generalisation is difficult at the cross-national level because there are too few societies to provide a full range of variation. At the same time, there are enormous disparities in terms of area, population, wealth, resources and military power between nominally independent, sovereign states. Is like being compared with like? Beyond such operational difficulties, it can be objected that genuine cross-national comparison is not possible because each society is a unique configuration, the product of specific historical circumstances. Its institutions, values and mores reflect a singular culture, which can only be comprehended in its entirety. Attempts at cross-national comparison are therefore held by some scholars to be at best procrustean and at worst misconceived.[21]

There is substance in this argument – any society is in some respects unique – but overstated, it becomes self-defeating. Why should the argument stop there, once the unique and non-comparable nature of societies is conceded? Each group, community or locality – indeed every individual – is also unique in at least some respects, and hence non-comparable. Any kind of generalisation not only becomes hazardous (which it often is) but impermissible; the outcome of the argument is absurdly restrictive and negative. The grain of good sense is that comparison must take into account the history and culture of the societies concerned. There must be sufficient similarity in relevant respects to allow sensible use of the analytical categories concerned.

To illustrate the point: Britain and the USSR are in many ways very unlike societies. Direct comparison of, say, the electoral process in Britain with that of the USSR is unlikely to be very instructive. As Lord Attlee once commented, "Soviet elections are a race with one horse". Competitive elections have different functions from such 'elections without choice'. Beyond pointing up the contrast, there is insufficient common ground for fruitful comparison, because the phenomena involved belong to different categories.[22] On the other hand, the Soviet experience of urbanisation and its effects might usefully be viewed in the context of other highly urbanised, industrial societies. Has large-scale urbanisation generated problems resembling those of Britain's cities, and how have policy-makers responded to them?[23] This might be a feasible line of comparative investigation between societies that are so different in other respects. The moral, perhaps, is that the researcher must choose the focus of comparison and the cases for review with care.

Concepts are of key importance in comparative research. So what are they? Put simply, a concept is a general term which represents all the phenomena in a particular class, whether these be material or abstract. The difference between the use of concepts in everyday language and those of academic enquiry is that the latter are (usually) defined more precisely both in themselves and in relation to each other, and tend to be at a higher level of generality.

Note that the test of any concept is not whether it is 'true' or 'real', but whether it generates promising theories. The record of Comparative Politics is littered with defunct concepts which have proved insufficiently fertile and perished through neglect.[24] Comparative political research does, however, require hard, conscious thinking about concepts, especially where cross-national study is involved because of the complications posed by differences of culture and language and the difficulties attending the collection and standardisation of data. As Dogan and Pelassy put it, questions full of meaning in an opinion poll carried out in England or Scandinavia may offend people in Japan and not translate at all into Arabic.[25]

In effect, the concepts used in comparative analysis need progressive elaboration and refinement to make them 'travel'. At the same time, as Sartori has noted, there is a temptation to stretch concepts, so as to accommodate more and more cases, but this ultimately erodes their analytical value.[26] Some concepts cannot travel far. As we saw, competitive and non-competitive elections belong in different categories; it makes little sense to lump them together. Concepts have to be applied carefully to cases. The idea of the two-party system applies only to a handful of countries (among them Britain, USA and New Zealand) and in each case involves considerable abstraction from reality. The 'two-party system' is not a straightforward description of British or American party politics. Rather, it suggests a model of party competition to which these countries tend (at times), while deliberately omitting a great deal of extraneous – or if you prefer, inconvenient – detail. The model, however, facilitates comparison of the British and American party systems: in what points they resemble and to what extent they differ from one another. It also provides a yardstick against which to measure changes within the party system of each country. Is the two-party system in Britain in decline?[27] Before we can judge, we need to be clear about the concept.

Concepts in Comparative Politics thus range from highly general ideas encompassing many cases or societies (such as 'modernisation'; 'industrial society'; 'authoritarian regimes') to those which are located in much more specific contexts (such as 'judicial review' or *proporz* democracy'). Sartori has termed this the ladder of abstraction, upon which a researcher must manoeuvre between general concepts of wide applicability ('political leadership') to narrow-gauge ones appropriate to the precise characteristics of the problems under study ('collective cabinet responsibility' in Britain; 'the *nomenklatura* system' in the USSR.)[28] Finding the right level is extremely important. As Alfred Grosser put it, 'One of the greatest difficulties in cumulative research is precisely to find the level of generalisation which permits the simultaneous avoiding of sterile theory on the one hand, of useless accumulation on the other.'[29] What progress has comparative research made in this task? We now turn to developments in the subject.

DEVELOPMENTS IN COMPARATIVE POLITICS

Thirty years ago Comparative Government was dominated by an approach that was predominantly descriptive, concentrating on the formal institutions of the state, legal and historical in tone. The approach was also configurative, emphasising what was distinctive to each system rather than drawing comparisons between them. In effect, the subject amounted to a collection of descriptions of foreign governments. This outlook became increasingly inappropriate to interpret contemporary political trends. The rise of fascist and communist regimes challenged the congenial assumption that evolutionary progress would sooner or later bring all societies into the liberal democratic fold: indeed they challenged the assumption that liberal democracy was the *summum bonum.* From within, the growth of big government, deeply enmeshed in economic management and welfare responsibilities was blurring the divide important in liberal theory between society and state. Internationally, the years after 1945 saw the transformation of the international state system by the Cold War. With the dismantling of empires, there emerged a Third World with the transition of dozens of colonial territories to (nominally) independent statehood. Particularly in the United States, with its super-power role after 1945, political scientists became increasingly aware that the conventional categories of Comparative Government were moribund and ill-suited to much of this unfolding reality.

Parallelling the behavioural movement within Political Science at large, a critical reassessment of Comparative Government began in the mid-1950s. In a sweeping critique which caught the mood, Roy Macridis condemned the traditional approach as 'essentially noncomparative, essentially descriptive, essentially parochial, essentially static, and essentially monographic.'[30] His clarion-call to revolt found a ready response. New concepts were created or borrowed from other branches of learning: Sociology, Anthropology, Psychology, Economics, Cybernetics. The advent of computers began to have a great impact, meeting the new passion for quantification and more 'rigorous' methods of enquiry. Novel schemes of classification proliferated. Practitioners felt that a new science of Comparative Politics was in the making. In 1966, Almond and Powell announced in the first sentence of their influential textbook that, 'during the last decade an intellectual revolution has been taking place in the study of comparative government.'[31]

The revolutionaries were offering new paradigms for old. Most significant of the new approaches were the General Systems model advocated by David Easton and the Structural-Functional approach associated with Gabriel Almond. It may be useful to indicate briefly the nature of each. Abbreviating drastically, Easton's approach might be conveyed in six main propositions:[32]

(i) the political life of a society may be conceived as a system, that is as a complex pattern of interdependent elements.

(ii) any system must have a boundary. Politics is defined by Easton as the 'authoritative allocation of values'. The boundaries of the political system encompass those activities more or less directly related to the making of binding decision for the entire society.

(iii) the political process involves the conversion of inputs (societal wants and demands) into outputs (decisions and policies) through the mechanisms of government. If the system is to be maintained, outputs must bear some relation to inputs over the long run.

(iv) The flow of inputs is regulated in a selective way by 'gatekeepers' (interest groups, political parties, mass media etc.). Inputs may be generated internally within the conversion processes ('withinputs').

(v) A political system requires inputs of support (taxes, participation and compliance) as well as demands. Support may be specific to particular policies or decision-makers, or more diffuse towards the institutions of the system as a whole. Without some level of diffuse support the system would ultimately collapse.

(vi) A political system has self-monitoring and self-regulating properties. As with electronic or biological systems, such feedback loops help the system to operate within a changing environment.

Easton's model is intentionally of a very abstract, almost metaphysical, character. It has been attacked on the count that it is difficult to derive practical guidance and benefit from a theory at such a high level of generality. The selection of relevant facts is made no easier and is arguably harder, because the definition of politics is so inclusive. Moreover, key variables like the extent of support for the political system are no easier to gauge with general systems theory than without it. The systems view of politics receives wide lip-service, for instance in the introductory chapters of textbooks, which then proceed with a resolutely configurative country-by-country approach. It is, perhaps, more helpful as a metaphor than as a practical method of analysis. It can direct attention to aspects of political behaviour that might otherwise be overlooked or ignored, for example sources of support or the articulation of demands in allegedly repressive regimes.

The main advocate of functionalist thinking in Politics has been Gabriel Almond, who synthesised Easton's system perspective with other ideas drawn from Anthropology and sociological theory.[33] All political systems from the simplest to the most developed, runs the argument, must perform a number of essential functions in order to persist. These functions are likely to be undertaken by different structures in different societies. There is no fixed relationship between particular structures and particular functions. The mistake of earlier theorists was to assume that there was (by supposing, for example, that law-making was the sole province of the legislature). Moreover,

Almond emphasised that some structures may perform more than one function: the Communist Party in the Soviet Union would seem to be involved with all the functions mentioned by Almond, but this would not preclude some role for other structures as well. His check-list of functions has varied somewhat over the years, but includes interest articulation, interest aggregation, rule formulation, rule implementation, rule adjudication, political socialisation, political recruitment and political communication. There are problems with the functional approach, but even a tenacious critic has conceded that the check-list of functions is useful.[34] Almond's work also has a strong developmental strain. He was particularly concerned to accommodate the politics of non-Western societies. Political systems are conceived across a gamut, from simple societies with little in the way of specialised political roles (an hereditary chief or council of tribal elders perhaps) to modernised societies which have complex, secularised and highly differentiated political structures (the United States or the Soviet Union). Needless to say, Almond drew an important contrast between democratic and totalitarian political systems, based on the extent of social pluralism ('sub-system autonomy') that is permitted.

Almond's objective, like that of Easton, was to create a model, global in scope, for analysing politics in any society that would be objective, standardised and culture-free. It is far from clear that he achieved this if the extent of critical reaction is any indication, though a number of country studies have been written along structural-functional lines. Among the criticisms that have been made are that the teleological assumptions of functionalism are at odds with the positivist claims of Almond's theory; that functionalist argument is circular and shows internal inconsistency; that the theory is culture-biased and that there are discrepancies in the number and performance of functions.[35] Neither structural-functionalism nor systems theory commanded full acceptance, and the claims of their adherents have become more muted in recent years.

Positivist aspirations have tended to shift towards economic or mathematical models, which treat politics as a form of exchange or coalition-forming activity.[36] The individual is conceived as rationally egoistic, striving to maximise personal satisfaction. The plausibility of this perspective is open to question. Does the accumulated evidence about the behaviour of political parties and electorates square with the postulate of rationally maximising voters and parties, which underpins Anthony Downs' influential work *An Economic Theory of Democ-*

racy?[37] Values are not bargaining chips, nor votes (always) a form of money. Moreover, violence and coercion seem just as prevalent in politics as peaceful accommodation and a willingness to split the difference. The main interest of political economy approaches is that, although direct applications may be limited, their indirect applications are wide: such models also appeal because they can be constructed in a more elegantly formal way than is the case with many other approaches to politics.

Ironically, perhaps, an alternative critique of mainstream Comparative Politics also derives from political economy, but in this case, that of Marxism. With the revival of Marxism in Western society since the late 1960s, a major project has been to achieve a generalised understanding of the formation of the world capitalist system. The works of Frank and Wallerstein attempt to trace the penetration of the world's societies by capitalist relations.[38] Various national-capitalisms, it is argued, can only be fully grasped and explained in terms of their location within, and inter-relationship with, an historical world-system, as it has developed over the course of the last half millenium from European origins to encompass the entire globe.[39] Cross-cultural and cross-national comparison is an intrinsic part of such an enterprise but the preoccupation of non-Marxists with the nation-state, *per se,* is regarded as misconceived. As Looker has commented, it is somewhat paradoxical that the positivist outlook of the comparative politics movement in the postwar years is now most fully articulated by Marxist scholars. In both cases, a central feature is the global reach and scope of the project, though their methodologies and substantive analysis are highly contradictory.[40]

Heroic positivists, whether Marxist, economic-modellers or system-theorists, have always been a minority, one suspects. More limited and mundane objectives have been the norm for most political scientists, and not without reason. Joseph LaPalombara forcefully expressed this point during the high summer of grand theory.[41] In his view, global theories were grossly premature even if they could ever be operationally helpful. Basic information was lacking on most aspects of government and politics in most societies. Political scientists are loathe to generalise, he said, about American politics (on which they have most information), 'while they will at the slightest stimulus generalise about large-scale societies in Africa, Asia and Latin America, concerning which our lack of historical and contemporary information is perhaps the most striking thing we can say.'[42] LaPalombara argued that partial theories (or middle range theories, in the words of the sociologist Robert Merton) were more likely to reap benefits. Put another way, research should concentrate on, say, corporatist trends in Norway. Propositions deriving from that should then be examined in the context of other societies. From this, a validated body of theory and empirical evidence about corporatism might accumulate. Whether this could ever be integrated with other partial theories into a more comprehensive and ultimately global form is a matter for the long term. LaPalombara's strictures were in any case running with the tide. Professional specialisation was rapidly producing segmentation of Comparative Politics into numerous research areas, and this trend continues. While there is little sign of wholesale integration, there are indications of partial theories based upon substantial cross-national validation emerging in some areas. Although Almond and Verba's landmark five-nation study *The Civic Culture* has been heavily criticised, it has also spawned numerous cross-national and cross-cultural studies of electoral behaviour, mass participation and citizen orientations towards politics. A fairly recent example would be the work of Samuel Barnes and his associates.[43] Another would be the projects headed by Ronald Inglehart into generational changes in politics.[44] If progress has been most striking in the (relatively) quantifiable area of electoral and mass survey research, substantial advances have been made in comparative understanding of institutional organisation and behaviour, for instance, through the work of the Consortium on Comparative Legislatures.[45]

Two examples might help to indicate the promise, as well as the challenge, of middle range theory. The relationship between elected politicians and senior civil servants, with its implications for policy-making, has been a focus of interest at least since Max Weber's seminal discussion of the problem early in this century. It can also be a source of humour, as witness the striking success of the *Yes Minister* television series. But how does the political culture of policy-making elites vary from country to country? To tackle this question, an ambitious study by Aberbach, Putnam and Rockman, among others, involved systematic interviews with more than 1400 senior civil servants and members of parliament in seven countries.[46] As the authors comment after a decade of travel and enquiry, if money is the mother's milk of politics, it is also the mother's milk of research. Though regarded by some as a hallmark of a subject with well-established research paradigms, such large-scale collaborative projects are still not typical of comparative political research. Individual scholarship remains the norm, though as the recent work of Mancur Olson shows, it need not shrink from large problems (in this case the reasons for the rise and decline of nations.)[47] Olson rudely assails the sacred cow of political stability, to which so much comparative analysis (and praise) has been devoted. He argues, by contrast, that social and political stability is inimical in the long run to economic growth. Stability fosters the emergence of special interests which form distributional coalitions, increasing social rigidities and impeding the efficient allocation of resources which, Olson argues, is necessary for sustained economic growth. The thesis is controversial, not least in its implications for policy, but is made with great clarity, deploying wide-ranging empirical evidence. Both of the foregoing studies are indisputably comparative in scope and execution. Each tackles a large cross-national canvas. Key concepts and hypotheses are outlined carefully, and 'operationalised' for use in different societies. Each shows ingenuity in devising suitable tests of its critical ideas. As the advocates of partial theory forewarn, a strategy appropriate to the research problem had to be developed. Other examples could be cited: the stimulating work of Valerie Bunce on executive succession and policy change in socialist and liberal democratic states;[48] the rigorous cross-national investigation of variations in welfare spending by H. L. Wilensky;[49] and, reflecting the shift of concern among political scientists from inputs (elections, interests, participation) to outputs (the policies and programmes that governments actually pursue), is Richard Rose's ambitious synthesis of the dynamics of governmental activity.[50] After the false dawning of global theory, the main advances in post-revolutionary Comparative Politics are being won through the systematic cross-national studies of the 'middle range'.

CONCLUSION: THE BALANCE SHEET

What is the balance sheet of change in Comparative Politics over the last thirty years? How much has changed and in what ways? Bearing in mind Macridis' critique of the mid-1950s, is Comparative Politics less parochial? On the whole, the answer is yes. The non-Western world undoubtedly receives more attention in teaching and research than formerly. Communist systems other than the Soviet Union are also more widely studied than hitherto.[51] But according to a recent survey of articles published in the main American professional periodicals devoted to Comparative Politics, West Germany, Britain and France top the list by a long way.[52] Moreover, although the old parochialism which simply ignored much of the world has diminished, it may have yielded to a new form, which compartmentalises on an area basis or into three separate worlds. The area approach — West European or East Asian or African or Latin American politics — has become popular with teachers and students over the last two decades. It has certain clear advantages: important characteristics (e.g. language or colonial rule) may be common to most of the societies involved. The risk is that the area approach becomes essentially configurative rather than comparative, and develops a distinctive research agenda dwelling on the special features and distinctive problems of the region.[53] This is entirely legitimate and is not to be condemned. The point here is that one kind of parochialism has been substituted for another. Furthermore, another aspect of professional parochialism remains substantially intact — that between Comparative Politics and International Relations. Specialists in each make frequent use of the system metaphor, at the heart of which is the notion of interdependence. Yet the interdependence of domestic and international politics is routinely ignored. The boundary between two sub-disciplines of Political Science remains a barrier to mutual communication.

Is Comparative Politics more 'comparative' than hitherto? Yes, up to a point though it depends on what you mean. There is greater conceptual awareness and more sophistication of method, sometimes too much so. As Sidney Verba aptly put it, 'In the old days, graduate students may have gone into the field as barefoot empiricists. Today they go equipped with elaborate systems models ... The barefoot empiricists didn't know where they might step; the recent students have trouble getting their feet on the ground.'[54] If comparative means cross-national, there have been some outstanding multi-country studies which have broken fresh ground and catalysed further research. Even so, the transformation of the subject can be exaggerated. The single-country study still flourishes. Moreover, the configurative country-by-country approach, although derided as outmoded, continues to be used in scores of undergraduate courses and textbooks in Britain and the United States. There are indications, in fact, of a revival of this approach over the last few years, as the patchy results of the revolution in Comparative Politics have become more apparent. Certainly, country-by-country courses are easier for teachers to organise and for students to comprehend.[55]

Is Comparative Politics less formalistic? Definitely. Legal-institutional formalism was one of the main charges laid against traditional writing on the subject. The lesson has been well taken. Remarkably little attention in post-revolutionary Comparative Politics has been given over to the analysis of the formal institutions of government. Constitutions are now a neglected area of comparative study. The professional journals reveal a very wide array of themes and issues, but a studied avoidance by scholars of formal institutions. In this respect, at least, the revolution in Comparative Politics succeeded only too well.[56]

Writing in the *Encyclopaedia of the Social Sciences* (published in 1968), Gabriel Almond characterised Comparative Politics as a movement within Political Science.[57] He did not see it as confined only to cross-national comparison, but sought to identify it with the other main 'reform movement' within Political Science of the 1950s and 1960s – the behavioural revolution. The aim was to enrich Political Science as a whole: to make it less parochial in scope, more inter-disciplinary in outlook, more scientific in method. Central to this positivist enterprise was the creation of a conceptual framework which would serve as a paradigm, to guide and integrate political research.

Almond's hopes lie clearly unfulfilled. In the post-revolutionary mood of the 1970s and 1980s, the quest for global theory in Comparative Politics has taken a back seat. The revolution succeeded in enlarging the scope of the subject. At times, indeed, the 'political' seemed in danger of disappearing altogether into the maw of Sociology, Psychology, Economics or whatever, as more and more factors were drawn into play (the fallacy of 'inputism', as Joseph LaPalombara termed it).[58] Comparative enquiry has in fact flourished, but amid a medley of concepts and strategies, rather than around a single paradigm. Partly this reflects a thriving concern. As Political Science came of age as a university based profession, an explosion of political knowledge resulted. Intense specialisation, increasingly aided by the data-handling power of computers, produced more knowledge (or to put it more cynically, more information) than could be accommodated within established frameworks. But it also reflects scepticism towards the notion of wider, all-embracing frameworks on the part of many in the profession. The present and perhaps permanent condition of Comparative Politics is a pluralism of methods, models and theories.

• NOTES

1. M. Dogan and D. Pelassy: How to Compare Nations (Chatham, New Jersey, Chatham House Publishers, 1984), 13-14.

2. L. M. Salamon: 'Comparative History and the Theory of Modernisation', World Politics, Vol. 23, No. 1 (1970), 83-103. Reprinted in P. Lewis, D. C. Potter and F. Castles (eds.): The Practice of Comparative Politics (Longman Open University, 1978), 339-360.

3. T. H. Rigby: Membership in the Soviet Communist Party, 1917-67 (Princeton: University Press, 1968).

4. D. Mayhew: Party Loyalty among Congressmen, 1947-62 (Cambridge, Mass.: Harvard University Press, 1966).

5. R. Macridis: The Study of Comparative Government (New York: Random House, 1955).

6. See article by R. Looker, 'Comparative politics: methods or theories?' in P. Lewis, et al., op. cit., 305-308. The issues raised by positivism are fully discussed in A. Ryan: The Philosophy of the Social Sciences (London: Macmillan, 1970).

7. L. Sigelman and G. H. Gadbois: 'Contemporary comparative politics: an inventory and assessment', Comparative Political Studies, Vol. 6, No. 3, (1983), 295-297. The authors undertook a content analysis of all articles appearing in Comparative Politics and Comparative Political Studies between 1968 and 1981. Single-country studies comprised 62% of the total, though over a third of these articles had some comparative elements.

8. G. K. Roberts: 'The explanation of politics: comparison, strategy and theory', in Lewis et al., op. cit., 289-290.

9. Ibid, 291.

10. See T. R. Dye: Politics, Economics and the Public (Chicago: Rand McNally, 1966). Also I. Sharkansky and R. I. Hofferbert: 'Dimensions of State Politics, Economics and Public Policy', American Political Science Review, Vol. 63, (1969), 867-879. This correlational approach is attacked in C. F. Cnudde and D. McCrone: 'Party Competition and Welfare Policies in the American States', American Political Science Review, Vol. 63, (1969), 858-866.

11. A. Lijphart: 'The comparable cases strategy in comparative research', Comparative Political Studies, Vol. 8, No. 1, (1975), 172-3.

12. C. Brinton: The Anatomy of Revolution (New York: Random House, 1965).

13. J. J. Richardson (ed.): Policy Styles in Western Europe (London: Allen and Unwin, 1982).

14. A. King: 'Ideas, institutions and the policies of governments: a comparative analysis', British Journal of Political Science, Vol. 3, Nos. 3, 4 (1973), 291-314, 409-424.

15. S. N. Eisenstadt: The Political Systems of Empires (New York: Free Press, 1963).

16. B. Moore Jr.: The Social Origins of Dictatorship and Democracy (London: Penguin Books, 1967). T. Skocpol: States and Social Revolutions (Cambridge: University Press, 1979). See the astringent critique of this genre by L. M. Salamon, op. cit.

44

17. S. Lipset and S. Rokkan (eds.): Party Systems and Voter Alignments: Cross-National Perspectives (New York: Free Press, 1967).

18. Cited in Dogan and Pelassy, op. cit., 6.

19. M. Duverger: Political Parties (London: Methuen, 1955).

20. D. W. Rae: The Political Consequences of Electoral Laws (New Haven: Yale University Press, 1967).

21. W. Dilthey: Meaning in History (London: Allen and Unwin, 1961). See also A. MacIntyre: 'Is a science of comparative politics possible?', reprinted in Lewis et al., op. cit., 266-286.

22. A direct comparison of the British and Soviet political systems has been attempted. See J. M. Gilison: British and Soviet Politics: legitimacy and convergence (Baltimore: Johns Hopkins Press, 1972). The best known instance of a 'most different' binary comparison is S. Huntington and Z. Brzezinski: Political Power – USA:USSR (New York: Viking, 1964).

23. J. Pallot and D. Shaw: Planning in the Soviet Union (Georgia: University Press, 1981).

24. W. J. Goode, cited in Dogan and Pelassy, op. cit., 23.

25. Dogan and Pelassy, op. cit., 11.

26. G. Sartori: 'Concept misformation in comparative politics', American Political Science Review, Vol. 54, (1970), 1033-53. Reprinted in Lewis et al., op. cit., 228-265.

27. For a consideration of this question, see M. Harrop: 'The Changing British Electorate', Political Quarterly, Vol. 53, (1982), 385-402.

28. Sartori, op. cit., 240-250.

29. Cited in Dogan and Pelassy, op. cit., 28.

30. Macridis, op. cit., 7-12.

31. G. Almond and G. B. Powell: Comparative Politics (Boston: Little Brown, 1966).

32. The most accessible version of Easton's ideas is in 'An approach to the analysis of political systems', World Politics, Vol. 10, (1957), 383-408. More elaborate restatements of the approach are in D. Easton: A Systems Analysis of Political Life (London: Wiley, 1965) and D. Easton: A Framework for Political Analysis (New Jersey: Prentice Hall, 1965).

33. Almond's ideas have been developed singly or with collaborators in numerous publications. The key source is probably G. Almond and J. S. Coleman (eds.): The Politics of the Developing Areas (Princeton: University Press, 1960). See also G. Almond and G. B. Powell: Comparative Politics, op. cit., 1966 (revised ed. 1978). For a sympathetic portrayal of the ideas of these and other innovators of the 'revolutionary' years, see M. Davies and V. A. Lewis: Models of Political Systems (London: Macmillan, 1971).

34. S. E. Finer: 'Almond's concept of 'The Political System': a textual critique', Government and Opposition, Vol. 5, No. 1, (1970), 3-21.

35. The literature for and against functionalism is vast. For a compact summary of its uses and abuses, see R. E. Jones: The Functional Analysis of Politics (London: Routledge and Kegan Paul, 1967). A very penetrating study is B. Barry: Sociologists, Economists and Democracy (London: Collier Macmillan, 1970).

36. See R. Curry and L. Wade: A Theory of Political Exchange (New Jersey:

Prentice Hall, 1968). Also T. A. Reilly and W. M. Sigal: Political Bargaining: an introduction to modern politics (San Francisco: W. H. Freeman, 1976), I. Budge and A. C. Fairlee: Voting and Party Competition (London: Wiley, 1976) and D. Robertson: A Theory of Party Competition (London: Wiley, 1976).

37. A. Downs: An Economic Theory of Democracy (New York: Harper and Row, 1957).

38. A. Gunder Frank: Dependent Accumulation and Underdevelopment (London: Macmillan, 1978). Also his: Crisis in the Third World (New York: Holmes and Meier, 1981), and I. Wallerstein: The Capitalist World Economy (Cambridge: University Press, 1979).

39. Looker, op. cit., 332.

40. Ibid.

41. J. LaPalombara: 'Macrotheories and microtheories in comparative politics', Comparative Politics, Vol. 1, (1968), 60-71.

42. Ibid, 63.

43. S. H. Barnes, M. Kaase et al., Political Action: Mass Participation in 5 Western Democracies (London and Beverley Hills: Sage, 1979).

44. Inglehart's work on post-material generational change has appeared in various publications. But see R. Inglehart: 'Post Materialism in an Environment of Insecurity', American Political Science Review, Vol. 75, No. 4, (1981).

45. The Consortium has published several volumes, but much of this and other research is synthesised in M. Mezey: Comparative Legislatures (Durham, N. Carolina: Duke University Press, 1979).

46. J. D. Aberbach, R. D. Putnam and B. A. Rockman: Bureaucrats and Politicians in Western Democracies (Cambridge, Mass.: Harvard University Press, 1981).

47. M. Olson: The Rise and Decline of Nations (New Haven: Yale University Press, 1982).

48. V. A. Bunce: Do New Leaders Make a Difference? (Princeton: University Press, 1981).

49. H. L. Wilensky: The Welfare State and Equality (Berkeley: University of California Press, 1975).

50. R. Rose: Understanding Big Government (London: Sage, 1984).

51. For a survey of contemporary texts and courses, see L. C. Mayer: 'Practising what we preach – comparative politics in the 1980s', Comparative Political Studies, Vol. 16, No. 2, (1983), 173-194.

52. Sigelman and Gadbois, op. cit., 286-287.

53. Ibid, 289-290.

54. S. Verba: 'Some dilemmas in comparative research', World Politics, Vol. 20 (1967), 117.

55. Mayer, op. cit., 186-191.

56. Sigelman and Gadbois, op. cit., 293. Coding articles for their substantive focus proved to be extremely difficult, but according to the authors' analysis, the proportion of studies dealing primarily with the basic structures of government (constitutions, legislatures, executive, administration, courts) was less than 7% of the total.

57. G. Almond: Entry under 'Comparative Politics', Encyclopaedia of the Social Sciences (1968).

58. J. LaPalombara, op. cit. See also G. D. Paige: 'The primacy of politics' in Lewis et al., op. cit., 361-371.

SELECT BIBLIOGRAPHY

The first four items are examples of current textbooks, chosen to illustrate the diversity of approaches. Then come a number of studies which are more restricted in scope but deal with aspects of comparative politics in a cross-national way. Finally, we include a recent book which deals with problems and concepts of comparison in a very lucid way.

G. Almond and G. B. Powell: Comparative Politics (Boston: Little Brown, Second edition, 1978).

S. Beer and A. Ulam: Patterns of Government (New York: Random House, Third edition, 1974).

G. Bertsch, R. P. Clark and D. M. Wood: Comparing Political Systems – power and policy in three worlds (New York: Wiley, 1978).

R. Hague and M. Harrop: Comparative Government (London: Macmillan, 1982).

G. Sartori: Parties and Party Systems (Cambridge: University Press, 1976).

M. Mezey: Comparative Legislatures (Durham, N. Carolina: Duke University Press, 1979).

V. Bunce: Do Leaders make a Difference? (Princeton: University Press, 1981).

A. Heidenheimer, H. Heclo and C. Adams: Comparative Public Policy (Macmillan: Second edition, 1983).

R. Rose: Understanding Big Government (London: Sage, 1984).

M. Olson: The Rise and Decline of Nations (New Haven: Yale University Press, 1982).

T. Skocpol: States and Social Revolutions (Cambridge: University Press, 1979).

M. Dogan and D. Pelassy: How to Compare Nations (New Jersey: Chatham House Publishers, 1984).

Political Sociology

Roger King

Even if they may agree on little else, most political sociologists accept that Political Sociology is concerned with the analysis of power. Bottomore, for example, in his recent book, *Political Sociology,* asserts that 'the principal object of Political Sociology should be the phenomenon of power at the level of an inclusive society, the relations between such societies, and the social movements, organisations and institutions which are directly involved in the determination of power.'[1] Similarly, Dowse and Hughes suggest that Political Sociology 'is concerned with understanding all the problems pertaining to power and its use in societal contexts . . .'[2] They reject a definition confining Political Sociology to the analysis of institutions, such as the state, although they recognise that in practice political sociologists are often interested in state-society relationships. A further specification of Political Sociology's domain that generally elicits agreement from its practitioners is that it is concerned with exploring the ways in which the social and the political are related. Runciman, for example, traces the emergence of Political Sociology to the relatively modern distinction between the political and the social in the history of ideas.[3] In turn, this is linked to the contrast between 'civil society' and the 'state' which developed with the spread of industrial capitalism and which, as Bottomore notes, imparted a greater efficacy to socio-economic forces than hitherto.[4] The polarity of the political and the social is found in the works of the early European political sociologists in the respective importance they attached to the 'democratic' and 'industrial' revolutions of the late eighteenth and nineteenth centuries. The abiding issues for Tocqueville, for example, concerned the social consequences of the emergence of democratic government,[5] although for others, noticeably Marx, the compelling subject was the development of capitalism and its class relations, processes which he regarded as reflected in political arrangements.[6] This difference in emphasis tended to be associated with contrasting interpretations of liberal democratic institutions, regarded either as 'spurious' and part of an ideological cover for class inequality that aimed at preventing progress towards 'true' participatory democracy, or as genuinely conferring and extending substantial rights and benefits to national citizenry.

The identification of 'power' as the central concept for Political Sociology and the claim that the interrelationship of the social and the political is its major concern are not particularly useful delimitations of Political Sociology's domain, and equally could be said to characterise other disciplines. Indeed, in recent years, political sociologists have constantly bewailed what they regard as the subject's fragmentation and lack of focus. At a Social Science Research Council Conference convened in the mid-1970s to consider the state of Political Sociology it was reported that 'there appeared little agreement about what topics should be covered and that there is no agreement concerning the intellectual framework of the discipline.' The Conference concluded that 'the state of Political Sociology both as a structure of analysis and as a subject for teaching and research is in a fairly bad state.'[7] An explanation for this state of affairs is offered by Dowse and Hughes in their suggestion that Political Sociology reflects and compounds the dissensus on scope and methods to be found in both Sociology and Political Science. They add that Political Sociology also possesses a schizophrenic institutional location, in some cases being taught within Sociology Departments and in others within Political Science Departments. In their view, the catholicism of the founding fathers of Political Sociology, (Tocqueville, Marx, Weber, Pareto, Mosca, Spencer), has been displaced by the organisational specialisation of academic labour in modern higher education institutions.[8]

The extent to which Political Sociology courses are connected to either a Sociology or a Political Science Department does appear to make a difference to what is taught. A survey of Political Sociology courses by Philip Abrams in the early 1970s revealed that courses provided by Political Science Departments are much more likely to pay attention to individual political behaviour, covering such topics as voting, participation, attitudes, socialisation and formal models of political systems and institutions, than those provided by Sociology Departments which tend to indicate an interest in radical socio-political change, (e.g. fascism, socialist revolutions), ideology, and the debate on the structure of power. However, Abrams concluded that this was more a matter of emphasis than alternative content.[9]

To a large extent these differences reflect the two major traditions in Political Sociology; the European and the American. The earliest tradition is the European and derives directly from the classical foundations of general sociology, i.e. the earliest sociologists, such as Marx, Weber, Pareto and Spencer, were political sociologists. It has concerned itself with grand theory or 'macro' issues, focusing particularly on the sources and effects of the great socio-economic changes, e.g. capitalism, the division of labour. Its legacy to contemporary Political Sociology is the recognition that patterns of social stratification and the economic structures of society are crucial sources of political institutions, and its elaboration of key concepts such as 'class', 'elite' and 'bureaucracy'. The American or 'behaviourist' tradition originates later, and became especially influential in the United States in the 1930s and 1940s. It may be said to differ from the European in three particular ways: (i) whereas the Europeans emphasised the 'macro', Americans studied the 'micro', or the social psychological aspects of politics. Alongside this, Lazarsfeld,[10] Berelson[11] and others pioneered techniques of participant observation, questionnaire survey, attitude tests, and generally sought methodological rigour; (ii) instead of making assumptions about the psychological aspects of politics, the Americans factually researched it and questions about socialisation and culture were answered by detailed research into the ways in which institutions such as the family and the media acted to create attitudes; and (iii) whereas the Europeans studied ruling classes or elites, American behaviourists, such as Lasswell[12] and Key,[13] focused on the 'ordinary man', and typical results that emerged from the case studies and surveys were descriptions of the range of factors that influenced ordinary voting decisions or affected political participation.[14]

In the 1950s and 1960s the American and European traditions came together in a mutually complementary way that gave Political Sociology for almost twenty years 'a purpose with a single-minded dedication.'[15] It rested on the assumed acceptability of existing liberal democracies and a search for their stabilisation, and brought together the micro, empirical concerns of the behaviourists and the theoretical and speculative notions of the Europeans. Claims of an identity crisis in Political Sociology in the last decade may be traced to the disintegration of this 'central purpose' in Political Sociology in the late 1960s as the limitations of the approach were exposed by the eruption in the West of more conflictual political events than assumed by the model and the consequent scrutiny by more radical, often Marxist, critiques that became more influential in the social sciences. In turn, the paradigmatic jostling and uncertainties in Political Sociology that followed, and the apparent success of a strong model in giving areas such as Urban

Sociology a renewed sense of direction, has led some to argue for a new unitary model for Political Sociology.[16] The question of whether this is an appropriate strategy will be considered later. First we examine the orthodoxy in Political Sociology that prevailed in the post-1950 period.

THE SOCIOLOGY OF DEMOCRACY, 1950-1970

A long-standing tension in Political Sociology arises from competing conceptions of democracy. Marxists regard 'democracy' as a class-based historical movement aimed at encouraging individuals to participate fully in those institutions that control their lives. 'Democratic elitists', however, such as Pareto,[17] Mosca,[18] Michels[19] and Schumpeter,[20] conceive 'democracy' in a more limited way, as a method for choosing betweeen political leaders competing for the people's vote in periodic elections. This latter perspective provides a key link between the European and American traditions in Political Sociology. Originating in European elite theory, democratic elitism became a strong influence within the behaviourist tradition, hence the attention devoted to election studies, but is most explicitly articulated in the voting studies of Lazarsfeld, Berelson and their associates in the 1940s.[21] It emerges from their findings that the long-held model of a well-informed, politically-aware citizenry carefully choosing between candidates at election time, rather in the way that price-sensitive 'economic man' chooses between consumer goods, was empirically untenable. Berelson and his colleagues sought to justify the relatively high levels of disinterestedness and unawareness they discovered in the electorate by arguing that a more 'realistic' and limited idea of democracy, as elite competition rather than full-participation, would indicate that apathy could be good for the political system: it prevented conflicts from becoming too acute, allowed defeat to be accepted gracefully, and provided the basis for change with continuity.[22]

These themes clearly linked to the wider concerns of European Political Sociology and the outcome was convergence in what we may term a Sociology of Democracy; its key figures were Seymour Martin Lipset, Stein Rokkan and Rhinehart Bendix. From the mid-1950s, Political Sociology on both sides of the Atlantic became marked by an academic orthodoxy which was characterised by two main assumptions: (i) that the liberal regimes in most of the western industrial nations were as democratic as one could reasonably expect and the issue was to identify how such regimes could be stabilised and their example furthered elsewhere; and (ii) that the social largely determines the political and that the answer to the issue identified in (i) lay in establishing the social causes or requisites of democracy. Two works of crucial influence were Almond and Verba's *The Civic Culture*,[23] which sought to demonstrate through cross-national surveys that democratic regimes were sustained by a 'civic' culture, operationalised as a mix of participatory/deferential attitudes in its citizenry, and Lipset's *Political Man*,[24] which additionally connected stable liberal democracies with industrial advance which, it was claimed, provided the resources and wealth to sustain regime legitimacy. A feature of the approach, however, was the limited version of democracy adopted — the 'democratic elitist' notion of elite competition in accordance with constitutional procedures. It seemed to set the main task for Political Sociology as the search for the causes of stability, rather than democracy *per se*, and in demonstrating how elite rule can be made acceptable to largely non-participatory masses.[25]

Institutional backing for this 'programme' came from a variety of sources, particularly the Committee on Political Sociology set up in 1960 by the International Sociological Association and presided over by Lipset. The major theme that informed the work of the Committee, and which found expression in Lipset and Rokkan's *Party Systems and Voter Alignments*,[26] was to account for variations in European party systems (and, by implication, political systems), by referring them back to the historical conflicts and cleavages faced by all advanced European societies, i.e. subject versus dominant cultures, churches versus secular governments, rural versus urban, and workers versus employers. The two fundamental questions that concerned Lipset and Rokkan were: (i) how, and in what way, do the cleavages and supports of wider stratification systems get translated into party and political forms? And, (ii) can party systems themselves be seen as an independent force over and above social and economic systems? The overarching concern, however, was to explain how a viable system of political decision-making is achieved in the face of the fissures and divisions of interest produced by industrialisation, with a crucial factor identified as the 'non-accumulation' and resolution of essentially non-bargainable cleavages, e.g. those centred on religion, language, culture, before these have the opportunity to overlay the essentially secular and bargainable cleavages between employers and workers over the distribution of goods in advanced capitalism. A feature of this work, reflecting the influence of American behaviourism, was its methodological sophistication, particularly the multivariate analysis of voting statistics.

A related, but somewhat subordinated, theme that emerged during this period, and found principally in the work of Bendix,[27] concerned an examination of the creation of national political communities through an extension of citizenship rights to the lower classes in exchange for their acceptance of the liberal democratic state. However, and in comparison with recent 'corporatist' theories (see later), the 'incorporation' of the masses was viewed only as positive, as stabilising regimes, and the constraints on political action by the disadvantaged that was also entailed were largely ignored. Furthermore, the implications of this work for theories of state power were never pursued, and during this period Political Sociology generally turned away from a concern with the state. In so doing it ignored increasing state interventions in modern society, particularly the economy, and was unprepared both for those social movements in the late 1960s that challenged state regulation and existing political arrangements, and for the theoretical assaults on the dominant orthodoxy that followed.

POLITICAL SOCIOLOGY IN THE 1970s AND 1980s

(a) The State

The eclecticism of current Political Sociology reflects a continuing recognition of the academic worth of the dominant orthodoxy as well as the stimulation and theoretical sophistication of what we may term 'the new Political Sociology'. A central feature of the latter is a concern with theorising the state, particularly relationships with socio-economic forces.[28] Although reflecting the increased influence of Marxism, the new critiques are critical of both conventional Marxism and orthodox Political Sociology. A rediscovery of the 'relative autonomy' of the 'political', for example, indicates dissatisfaction with the vulgar economic determinism of the former and the sociological reductionism of the latter. A striking feature of contemporary Political Sociology is the extent to which Marxists and non-Marxists frequently share an interest in similar problems, such as the extent to which the development of the welfare state and the growth of labour parties and trade unions constitute advance for the working-class. The increased influence of 'class conflict' rather than 'logic of capital' models in

Marxism, which allows a greater scope for 'human action' than functional economism, and the sophistication of analyses of the state that have ensued, (e.g. Gough,[29] Holloway and Picciotto,[30] Jessop,[31] and Offe[32]), indicate convergence with an 'older' Weberian interest in political forms that was largely overlooked in Political Sociology in the 1950s and 1960s. This is exemplified in critiques of Marx's theory of the state which saw it as in fairly strict 'correspondence' with economic processes, or 'modes of production'. Structural Marxists, such as Althusser[33] and Poulantzas,[34] assert that the 'mode of production' is a complex whole, comprised of several distinct 'levels': the economic, political, cultural and theoretical/scientific. All have a 'relative autonomy' — the political, for example, does not simply reflect the economic — and a mode of production is characterised by the particular articulation of these levels. Hindess,[35] Hirst,[36] Anderson[37] and others go further in questioning the correspondence of modes of production with forms of political regime and have challenged 'historicist' assumptions in Marxism, the idea of unilinear, law-governed lines of development. For them the task is explaining the interconnection of different elements or levels within a particular type of society and state. These concerns are associated with a renewed interest in the comparative historical analysis of social change. Although in part stimulated by Barrington Moore's, *Social Origins of Dictatorship and Democracy,*[38] published in the late 1960s, and which paid particular attention to the influences of class, especially agrarian relations, recent scholarship places greater emphasis on the part played by state power, war and the location of nation-states within world systems in explaining crucial historical change. A key work is Theda Skocpol's *States and Social Revolutions.*[39] This seeks to account for the French, Russian and Chinese revolutions by supplementing class analysis with a view of the state's role as an autonomous structure, ' . . . with a logic and interests of its own not necessarily equivalent to, or fused with, the dominant class in society or the full set of member groups in the polity.'[40] Skocpol shows clearly that the political crises that launched the revolutions in these countries were direct expressions of contradictions centred in the structures of old-regime states and did not simply reflect social interests and forces.

(b) Interest intermediation

Attention to state-society connections has coincided with increased analysis of relationships between organised groups and the polity. A major theme is the dilemma that confronts many pressure groups: whether to achieve a close working relationship with authority or not. A number of typologies have been constructed that distinguish between groups in this way: organisations are contrasted according to the degree to which they are *established* in the eyes of decision-makers;[41] to the extent to which they are *legitimised* in the eyes of the elites;[42] whether they seek strategically to be *outsiders* or *insiders*;[43] or whether they are regarded by government as *helpful* or *unhelpful*.[44] A central idea is that access to decision-makers is governed by certain 'rules of the game'. These 'rules' have to be negotiated and tend to operate against radical and/or militant groups.[45]

A more specialised body of theory has also developed to account for the way in which certain interests, primarily economic, are represented to government. This is the theory of 'corporatist intermediation' (and should be distinguished from 'corporatist' theories of forms of economy, e.g. Winkler's[46]); it stems, in part at least, from dissatisfaction with models of pluralist interest intermediation found in the political sociological orthodoxy of the 1960s.[47] Corporatism (ideal typically) is pictured as a system of interest intermediation – the term 'intermediation' being preferred to 'representation' to indicate the mutual and symbiotic relationships between groups and government – which differs from pluralism in that:

> ... the constituent units are organised into a limited number of singular, compulsory, non-competitive, hierarchically ordered and functionally differentiated categories, recognised or licensed, if not created, by the state and granted a deliberate representational monopoly within their respective categories in exchange for observing certain controls of the selection of leaders and the articulation of demands and supports.[48]

This view, expressed by Schmitter in Schmitter and Lehmbruch's *Trends Towards Corporatist Intermediation,* is regarded as particularly appropriate as a description of the relationships with the state enjoyed by many large socio-economic groups, e.g. the CBI or TUC in Britain, but also stresses the high degree of mutual co-operation between such groups. Recently, corporatist theory has become explicitly articulated with class theory; Crouch,[49] Panitch[50] and Offe,[51] for example, explore corporatism as a device for controlling working class demands. This follows from the necessity for stability and regulation in advanced capitalist economies, which are doubtfully provided by parliamentarism and pluralism with its 'irrationalities' and periodic concessions to popular demands. Nevertheless, whilst the major value of corporatist ideology is its stress on the 'harmonisation of interests' for national goals, which makes it especially attractive to social democratic govern-ments, in effect corporatist arrangements may be characterised by a high degree of instability and the inability of leaders to control members, particularly in the crucial area of incomes policy.[52]

(c) Political implications of changes in class structure

Changes in class structure, particularly the growth of the 'new middle-class' (managers, white-collar workers, salaried professionals), also have continued to be considered by political sociologists for their possible implications for political structures. A specific issue that taxes both Marxists and non-Marxists is whether the middle-class is a putative ally or foe for socialism. Middle-class support for socialist parties, for example, tends to be subject to two contrasting interpretations. One, associated with Marxism, asserts that it reflects a definite shift to the left in the centre of political gravity as a result of a two-fold process: first, the increasing 'proletarianisation' of many white-collar positions, manifested in loss of authority, job security, income and status;[53] and, second, a heightened radicalism by well paid professional and intellectual employees whose opposition to existing patterns of power is engendered by the dissemination of critical thinking in higher educ-ation and the growth of public service occupations which foster hostile attitudes to the market individualism of competitive capitalism.[54] An alternative perspective, put forward by Crewe *et al.*,[55] for example, posits a more benign possibility for liberal democracy as a result of the erosion of the link between occupational class and party partisanship. An increase in middle-class Labour voting is regarded as symptomatic of a less ideological form of politics in which electoral behaviour is charac-terised by increasing 'instrumentality' and the political parties judged in terms of their efficiency and effectiveness, particularly on economic issues. Both interpretations appear to have some support in the electoral data.[56]

We should note, however, that little work has been undertaken on the middle-class right in politics, although there are some signs that this is being remedied.[57]

(d) Urban Political Sociology

The resurgence of interest in theories of the state has also helped to stimulate interest in the Political Sociology of urban areas. Of particular importance is the work of Castells[58] which stresses that the 'specificity' of the 'urban' derives from its function in the social reproduction of labour power, i.e. urban areas in advanced capitalist societies are basically organised around the provision of collective goods for consumption. 'Collective consumption' refers to those services, such as housing and education, when these are provided by the state, and are distinguishable from commodity forms of commercially organised consumption. According to Castells, the large-scale organisation and 'politicised' form of collective consumption processes provide the inter-subjective basis for the development of social movements by those in receipt of such services. Castells' approach has been largely developed in the context of French urban politics and its more general applicability is not clear.[59] However, Castells' analysis is usefully developed in Britain by Dunleavy to account for the influence of housing and transport locations on voting.[60] An additional element in Dunleavy's work is the notion of 'consumption sectors', which refers to the fragmentation of individual and collective consumption models in certain sectors, e.g. housing, so that salient political cleavages emerge based on them, e.g. that between private homeowners and public housing tenants.

Weberian Political Sociology also explores the political implications in local areas of class situations other than those deriving from occupational position. Rex and Moore, in their study of immigrant groups in Birmingham in the 1960s theorised 'housing classes' as significant political agents.[61] More recently, Saunders has argued that homeowners possess a property that is usable for material reward which gives them a class position distinct from both those that rent their accommodation (private and public) and land-developers. These cleavages are reflected in political action, such as the existence of a specific 'ratepayers' interest in local elections.[62]

(e) Culture and Capitalism

Contemporary Political Sociology displays an increasingly marked interest in notions of 'culture' and the political implications of changes in social values and motivations. For both 'left' and 'right' in Political Sociology a source of major crisis for capitalism is constituted by the decline in 'the protestant ethic'. From within the 'critical theory' school of Frankfurt Marxism, for example, Habermas[63] draws attention to 'legitimation crises' in advanced capitalism that stem from the erosion of pre-capitalist or traditional bases of social integration, e.g. religion, which are essential to capitalism because it does not generate its own basis of legitimation and integration beyond the market. Furthermore, these are replaced by universalistic value systems which create 'new needs' and new dissatisfaction with the system. Habermas suggests that modern political systems are entering a situation where a new level of legitimacy is required, characterised by 'open knowledge' and a real process of 'open discourse' and morality.

The similarity of this analysis to Daniel Bell's account of the *Cultural Contradictions of Capitalism,*[64] written from a 'liberal-conservative' position, is striking. Bell also claims that the cultural sphere in 'post-industrial society' has become less a source of restraint and discipline – instilling norms of 'career achievement' and 'deferred gratification' that are necessary for capitalist production if not for capitalist consumption – than an area of self-realisation and gratification. It is characterised by an 'unrestrained modernism' and 'hunger for experience' that threatens the moral and economic basis of bourgeois society.

Bell's and Habermas' works usefully draw attention to the distinctive cultural orientations of recent social movements. The concepts 'culture' and 'cultural reproduction' may be more fruitful than narrower notions of 'political socialisation' and, as Bottomore notes, 'has the great merit of emphasising that the ideas and values shaping political action are not necessarily emphasised in an overtly political form and of relating such ideas and values to the whole social structure.'[65] Other writers, too, such as Bordieu,[66] and Offe,[67] have outlined how apparently 'unpolitical' cultural systems must be seen as an important element in political domination.

CONCLUSION

Political Sociology today looks very different from that of fifteen or twenty years ago. An orthodoxy centred on a Sociology of Democracy has been replaced by what some may regard as a disconcerting disunity and confusion. Thus political sociologists have sought a new unity although it is questionable that the strength and purpose in a discipline stems from a unitary model or paradigm. Jary,[68] for example, argues that a 'closed problematic' is the situation of a conservative or merely 'technical' science, or even a dogmatic one. He maintains that Political Sociology is a better critical science than it was in 1960 and that there are major increments to flexibility and understanding from a plurality of perspectives. Furthermore, the subject's current multi-paradigmatic character closely reflects, and helps to explain, existing political realities which are complex and conflictual.

Finally, perhaps we should recognise, with Bottomore, that Political Sociology is 'only a convenient descriptive title for a specific domain of investigation, a set of theoretical problems, which could perfectly well be referred to by some other name.'[69] We should note, too, that much of Political Sociology's purpose is constituted by political events and that political sociologists should consider what are the most important practical issues in the closing decades of the twentieth century and represent them in thought.

● NOTES

1. T. Bottomore: Political Sociology (London: Hutchinson, 1979), 7.

2. R. Dowse and J. Hughes: Political Sociology (London: Wiley, 1972), 7.

3. W. Runciman: Social Science and Political Theory (Cambridge: Cambridge University Press, 1969), 22.

4. Bottomore, op. cit., 8.

5. A. de Tocqueville: The Old Regime and the French Revolution (N.Y.,: Doubleday, 1955).

6. K. Marx: A Contribution to the Critique of Political Economy (London: Lawrence and Wishart, 1964).

7. See P. Abrams, 'On Political Sociology', Appendix C to the Report, (1974), 2.

8. Dowse and Hughes, op. cit., 2.

9. Abrams, op. cit., 4.

10. P. Lazarsfeld, B. Berelson and H. Gandet: The People's Choice (New York: Sloan and Pearce, 1944).

11. B. Berelson, P. Lazarsfeld and W. McPhee: Voting (N.Y.,: Columbia U.P., 1954).

12. H. Lasswell: Politics: Who Gets What, When, How (N.Y.,: Meridian Books, 1958).

13. V. Key: Public Opinion and American Democracy (New York: Knopf, 1961).

14. An early seminal work of note was S. Rice: Quantitative Methods in Politics (New York: Knopf, 1928).

15. Abrams, op. cit., 5.

16. See, for example, R. Dowse, 'Towards a Reconceptualisation of Political Sociology', paper presented to the Political Sociology Panel at the Political Studies Association's Annual Conference, University of Exeter, April, 1980. A revised version of this paper will be published shortly in Teaching Politics.

17. V. Pareto: Treatise on General Sociology (London: Dover Publications, 1963).

18. G. Mosca: The Ruling Class (N.Y.,: McGraw-Hill, 1939).

19. R. Michels: Political Parties (N.Y.,: Free Press, 1966).

20. J. Schumpeter: Capitalism, Socialism and Democracy (London: Allen and Unwin, 1976).

21. Lazarsfeld et al., op. cit.; Berelson et al., op. cit.

22. Berelson et al., ibid.

23. G. Almond and S. Verba: The Civic Culture (Boston: Little, Brown, 1965).

24. S. Lipset: Political Man (London: Mercury Books, 1963).

25. Abrams, op. cit., 5.

26. S. Lipset and S. Rokkan: Party Systems and Voter Alignments (London: Collier-Macmillan, 1967).

27. R. Bendix: Nationbuilding and Citizenship (N.Y.,: Wiley, 1964).

28. We should not assume that 'orthodox' Political Sociology entirely neglected the state. See, for example, Bendix, ibid.

29. I. Gough, 'State Expenditure in Advanced Capitalism', New Left Review, 92, July-August, (1975), 53-92.

30. J. Holloway and S. Picciotto (eds.),: State and Capital (London: Arnold, 1978).

31. B. Jessop, 'The Transformation of the British State Since 1945', in M. Castells and R. Scase (eds.): The State in Western Europe (London: Croom Helm, 1979).

32. C. Offe, 'The Theory of the Capitalist State and the Problem of Policy', in L. Lindberg (ed.): Stress and Contradiction in Modern Capitalism (Lexington, Mass.: Lexington, 1975).

33. L. Althusser: Lenin, Philosophy and Other Essays (London: New Left Books, 1971).

34. N. Poulantzas: Political Power and Social Classes (London: New Left Books, 1973).

35. B. Hindess and P. Hirst: Modes of Production and Social Formation (London: Macmillan, 1977).

36. P. Hirst: Social Evolution and Sociological Categories (London: Allen and Unwin, 1976).

37. P. Anderson: Lineages of the Absolutist State (London: New Left Books, 1974).

38. B. Moore: Social Origins of Dictatorship and Democracy (London: Allen Lane, 1967).

39. T. Skocpol: States and Social Revolutions (Cambridge: Cambridge University Press, 1979).

40. Skocpol, ibid.

41. K. Newton: Second City Politics (Oxford: Oxford University Press, 1976).

60

42. M. Kogan: Educational Policy Making (London: Allen and Unwin, 1975).

43. W. Grant, 'Insider Groups, Outsider Groups, and Interest Group Strategies in Britain', Working Paper No. 19, Department of Politics, University of Warwick, (1978).

44. J. Dearlove: The Politics of Policy in Local Government (Cambridge: Cambridge University Press, 1973).

45. P. Saunders: Urban Politics (London: Hutchinson, 1979).

46. J. Winkler, 'Corporatism', Archives Europeénes de Sociologie, 17 (1976), 100-136.

47. For a good summary of the pluralist literature see S. Lukes: Power: A Radical View (London: Macmillan, 1974).

48. P. Schmitter, 'Still the Century of Corporatism?' in P. Schmitter and G. Lehmbruch (eds.): Trends Toward Corporatist Intermediation (London: Sage, 1979), 7-52.

49. C. Crouch, 'The Changing Role of the State in Industrial Relations in Western Europe', in C. Crouch and A. Pizzorno (eds.): The Resurgence of Class Conflict in Western Europe Since 1968 (London: Macmillan, 1978).

50. L. Panitch, 'The Development of Corporatism in Liberal Democracies', in P. Schmitter and G. Lehmbruch, op. cit., 119-146.

51. Offe, op. cit.

52. Jessop, op. cit.

53. G. Carchedi: On the Economic Identification of Social Classes (London: Routledge, 1978).

54. J. Habermas: Legitimation Crisis (London: Heinemann, 1976).

55. I. Crewe et al., 'Partisan Dealignment in Britain', 1964-1974, British Journal of Political Science, Volume 7 (1977), 129-131.

56. D. Jary, 'A New Significance for the Middle-Class Left?', in J. Garrard et al. (eds.): The Middle-Class in Politics (Farnborough: Saxon House, 1978), 133-182.

57. R. King and N. Nugent: Respectable Rebels (Sevenoaks: Hodder and Stoughton, 1979).

58. M. Castells: The Urban Question (London: Arnold, 1977).

59. P. Saunders, op. cit.

60. P. Dunleavy: Urban Political Analysis (London: Macmillan, 1980).

61. J. Rex and R. Moore: Race, Community and Conflict (Oxford: Oxford University Press, 1967).

62. P. Saunders, op. cit.

63. J. Habermas, op. cit.

64. D. Bell: The Cultural Contradictions of Capitalism (London: Heinemann, 1975).

65. Bottomore, op. cit., 84.

66. P. Bordieu, 'Cultural reproduction and social reproduction', in R. Brown (ed.): Knowledge, Education and Cultural Change (London: Tavistock, 1971), 71.

67. C. Offe, 'Political Authority and Class Structures', International Journal of Sociology, Volume 2 (1972), 73-105.

68. D. Jary, 'Political Sociology and the Recent Epistemology of Feyerabend and Habermas', paper given to the British Sociological Association's/Political Studies Association's Political Sociology Study Group, London School of Economics, December, 1979.

69. Bottomore, op. cit., 135.

SELECT BIBLIOGRAPHY

T. Bottomore: Political Sociology (London: Hutchinson, 1979).

R. Dowse and J. Hughes: Political Sociology (London: Wiley, 1972).

P. Dunleavey: Urban Political Analysis (London: Macmillan, 1980).

R. King (ed.): Capital and Politics (London: Routledge & Kegan Paul, 1983).

P. Saunders: Urban Politics (London: Hutchinson, 1979).

P. Schmitter and G. Lehmbruch (eds.): Towards a Theory of Corporatist Intermediation (London: Sage, 1979).

Urban Politics

Michael Goldsmith

Like Political Sociology, the subject matter of Urban Politics has changed considerably in scope and emphasis in recent years. Ten years ago only those teachers most heavily influenced by the American literature on community power and governmental outputs[1] would have talked about urban politics, and most would probably have settled for Local Government as the title of the course they were teaching. Today the field has attracted some of the best people working in the social sciences with important contributions from not only Political Science but also Sociology,[2] Geography,[3] History,[4] and Economics.[5] Marxist and neo-Marxist, Weberian, pluralist and elitist, as well as descriptive and barefoot empiricist writers are all to be found in the literature. For our purposes, the subject is best discussed under a number of headings, beginning with a review of theory and urban politics.

THEORY AND URBAN POLITICS

Developments in theory, in the form of the community power debate in the American literature, provided the initial revival of academic interest in local government and politics, both in the United States and Britain. The work of Dahl and Hunter in the late fifties provided hundreds of replicative studies and stimulated a new generation of British political scientists to look anew at the then largely descriptive and institutional field of local government. Many of the prominent writers currently working in the urban field, such as Bulpitt, Hampton, Hill, Jones, Lee, Newton, Saunders, Stanyer and Young[6] cut their academic teeth by exploring a little of 'the real world' of local politics, largely inspired by the ever increasing flow of literature across the Atlantic. Whilst few British authors replicated the American studies,[7] their work provides a staple diet for much of our empirical understanding of urban politics and provided the foundation on which subsequent work could build.

As I have noted elsewhere,[8] the community power debate focused attention on *who* makes the decisions in urban politics and the extent to which decisions are controlled by the few (the elite) or can be influenced by many (the pluralist alternative). The work also highlighted important issues, such as the distinction between decisions and nondecisions as well as ideas about such key concepts as power, influence, authority and control. Issues such as the nature of local decision-making elites; the process of elite recruitment, formal and informal holders of power, and particularly the influence of business interests on local politics were all central to the community power debate. However, in the end, political scientists increasingly saw the sterility of the debate and turned their attention to the outputs issue, seeking to ask 'what difference it makes who governs.'[9]

In seeking to answer the question, the dominant conceptual approach has been that of systems analysis, with political scientists particularly utilising the approach of David Easton. From this perspective, urban politics are seen as the means by which the urban political system (in most cases, local governments) reacts to changes in its social, economic, political and physical environment or seeks to adapt that environment. British writers using this approach include such authors as Young, Stanyer and Stewart,[10] but its main use has been in the American literature, especially that of the early and mid-seventies.[11]

Despite the utility of systems analysis as a heuristic device for organising and identifying variables, as well as suggesting relationships between them, systems theory is not really adequate as explanatory theory. Furthermore, the model's generality makes it largely empirically untestable, a weakness it shares with other theorists as we shall see. Lastly, the findings of many of those who employed the model suggested a strong measure of environmental rather than political determination of urban outputs. Socio-economic variables such as class, population size, density and so on, were seen as statistically better indicators of the kind and level of urban service provision than were political variables such as election turnout or the complexion of political control in a local authority. This weakness encouraged a number of writers in both Political Science and in Sociology to stress the role of individual actors (urban managers) in determining urban political outcomes.

Political scientists who have stressed the importance of individual political actor's perceptions of problems and his dispositions to deal with them (his political ideology or assumptive world) include such authors as Boaden, Dearlove and Young.[12] But the leading proponent of the urban managerialist thesis has undoubtedly been the sociologist Ray Pahl.[13] Concerned with explaining spatial inequalities in the city (a topic also of great interest to urban political geographers such as Harvey, Cox and Smith),[14] Pahl stressed the importance of the values and goals held by various 'urban managers', a category including not only councillors and officials, but also other local actors such as estate agents, building society managers and local businessmen. In his original formulation, Pahl was not clear on how these managers were to be defined and their power assessed and he also seriously underestimated the extent to which both market forces and the activities of central government seriously constrained the managers' actions. In subsequent reformulations, Pahl has stressed the managers' role in resource allocation, but recognised their limited control over resource availability.[15]

The main challenge to the urban managerialist model has come from Marxist and neo-Marxist approaches, most notably those writing in Urban Sociology, such as Castells, Offe, Pickvance and Saunders. One political scientist who has developed and applied Castells' 'collective consumption' approach to Urban Politics is Dunleavy, in his important text *Urban Political Analysis*.[16] This book is essential reading for all students interested in Urban Politics. Not only are Castells' ideas developed, but the book contains Dunleavy's own ideas about the national basis of urban political change, and the part played by local politics in that process. Particularly interesting are his short contributions on such topics as public service unions; land use planning; central-local government relations, the role of professionals in urban service provision and the relations between local authorities and the private sector.

Much of what Dunleavy has to say still requires further empirical verification, but the book remains a challenging and stimulating contribution. Another in a similar vein is Saunders' *Urban Politics: a sociological interpretation*,[17] which reviews and develops recent Weberian and neo-Marxist contributions, particularly those of Offe, and attempts to apply them to his own case study of Croydon. Though the case study and theoretical parts of the book do not fit together as well as one would like, Saunders' book parallels Dunleavy's work, yet remains in the traditional, localist vein.

Both Saunders and Dunleavy, however, stress the *interdependence* of national and local political processes and are rightly critical of the earlier writers who tended to see local authorities (and hence urban politics) as largely autonomous entities (a perspective encouraged by systemic models) operating independently of the political world around them. Over the last five years, this view of urban politics is one which has correctly been modified, though at times not without overstressing the extent to which local discretion has been eroded by the centre. Though the events following Mrs. Thatcher's election in 1979 give credence to such a view, the tactics and policies of Mr. Heseltine and the Department of Environment are so recent as to constitute an abrupt and fundamental change in the relationship between central government and local authorities, which is a theme to which we shall return later.

A last, somewhat weaker, strand of theoretical writing in Urban Politics is what might be called local level corporatism. Drawing on the ideas of recent corporatist writing, authors such as Rhodes, Flynn as well as Saunders and Cawson,[18] have applied the corporatist model both at the local level and to some of the national debates about local government. Again recent events have tended to undermine somewhat this trend in theoretical writing, though the most fruitful development remains one which could hopefully fuse the best elements of corporatist and neo-Marxist writings.

THEMES FOR ANALYSIS

If there have been considerable developments in urban political theory, there have also been significant contributions of a more empirical nature. Earlier studies, from Jones and Hampton through to Newton, focused most heavily on the input side of local politics and the nature of formal political decision-making at the local level. Since the early/ mid-seventies, three or four new themes have dominated empirically based work; output studies, seeking to explain variations in service performance; policy studies, with an emphasis on housing, land use planning, inner city deprivation and community development; central-local government relations, with the large Social Science Research Council funded initiative dominating the area, and the problem of fiscal stress in the city. Each is reviewed briefly in turn:

Output Studies

By comparison with North American and European counterparts, British political scientists by and large remain innumerate and unwilling to utilise computing aids to the maximum. This difference in part explains why there are so few output studies of the statistical kind associated with such American writers as Dye, Sharkansky and Hoffer-bert and the numerous graduate studies of local authority outputs.[19] Economists have made a number of contributions to the British literature,[20] but the main works remain that of people like Alt, Boaden, Davies and Stanyer,[21] though an important contribution is expected from Sharpe and Newton.[22]

The key issue raised by these output studies is whether or not politics matter when we seek to explain variations in the level of goods and services provided by local authorities. The American literature largely suggests that political factors are relatively unimportant in such explanations, with social, demographic and economic variables 'explaining' statistically the lion's share of the variations in performance. Thus, factors such as population size, population density, percentage of unfit housing, tax base (or rateable value in Britain) are more important determinants of local authority service provision than are such factors as voting turnout or the political complexion of the authority.

By contrast, however, the British literature generally finds that political variables are important, as does some of the European and Scandinavian work.[23] Certainly party control consistently emerges as an important variable, with Labour authorities being larger spenders generally and favouring social services such as housing, education and welfare. Conservative authorities spend less and generally prefer to spend more on the protection services such as fire and police.

Common sense suggests that such findings are hardly surprising. We would expect local authorities with large populations, high population densities, poor housing conditions or more resources to spend more on service provision generally, either because they have to (that is, the need for services is very high) or else they have the resources (especially finance) to do so. So the fact that demographic or economic variables are statistically more important in explaining service variations than are political variables should be expected. Needs or demands for services, as well as the resources to provide them, will probably be the prime indicators which councillors of all complexions will consider first, with their own political considerations following. Councillors, however, not only have to perceive the need for a service and have the resources to pay for it, but they also have to be *disposed* to provide the service, and disposition will reflect their political complexion.

In part this issue reflects one of the problems of output studies generally. However good the model or the data used, the amount of variation explained statistically remains low. Political indicators are generally difficult to find, but even the financial data normally used to measure service provision (expenditure per head) both fails to measure service quality and is normally limited to a single year's expenditure figures, thus failing to take into account variations in expenditure brought about by abnormal conditions. Though attempts have been made to deal with the quality problem and to undertake time series analyses, these are still not generally available in the literature, and the difficulties with political variables remain. Though we can expect a number of interesting contributions employing the quantitative methods associated with output studies, it seems doubtful whether they will make a substantial contribution to the future literature, if only because of these persisting difficulties and of those associated with the interpretation of data which require more qualitative, subjective work which may be less suited to statistical analysis.

Policy Studies
The need for more qualitative approaches to the analysis of local authority outputs provided an impetus for the Urban Politics literature to move in the direction of policy studies generally. Urban policy studies, like all policy studies, can be classified essentially under three headings: policy making; policy implementation and policy evaluation.

Whilst output studies have generally reviewed service provision across a wide range of services, urban policy studies have focused on a specific service usually as provided within a limited number of local authorities. The approach is essentially qualitative, involving detailed case studies of the service within one or more authorities. If the focus is on how policy for a particular service is made, the study will probably include some review of the interactions between the centre and the locality, as well as an analysis of national policy, if only to provide the context within which local policy is made. Housing and land use planning provide particularly good examples of this kind of work.[24] One important point to notice about these studies is their essentially interdisciplinary nature — Politics is but only one subject contributing to urban policy studies, and economists, sociologists, historians and geographers have all made important contributions to the urban policy literature.

Much of this literature has been concerned with the role played by individual actors and institutions in the policy-making process (in part the urban managerial thesis) and with attempting to see how far local authorities can manage their policy environment or are constrained by it. The work of political scientists such as Dearlove, Elkin and Young all strongly suggest that individual actors such as councillors and officials have considerable influence over policy, but that of sociologists such as Harloe as well as Paris *et al.*, and of Marxists generally, are more critical. At least, as Pahl argued in his reformulation of the urban managerial thesis, local councillors and officials may well be able to influence the *distribution* of scarce resources — for example by giving planning permissions or allocating council houses — but have very little control over the *acquisition* of resources to redistribute.

Two other features are prominent in much of this policy-making literature. First, there is the sense of how complex the policy-making process is, even for what at first sight might appear to be a simple policy question. Private interests, public sector quangos, voluntary associations, local authorities, central government departments and beyond to the EEC all become involved in developing (and subsequently implementing) a specific policy. The task of understanding how a policy is established is far more difficult than even the relatively sophisticated issue orientated pluralist writers, such as Dahl *et al.*, of the late fifties and early sixties, would have us believe. Reconstructing the policy-making process for a specific policy arena has become enormously difficult, a problem not made easier by statutory and other limitations on access to materials.

The second feature of importance is the sense of how interdependent all the elements in the policy-making process have become. In part, the argument is that, very broadly, most policy arenas, and thus most policy-making, are dominated by a national policy community, individual members of which are drawn in depending on what policy arena or issue is under discussion. Central government produces its policies, often as a result of extensive consultation with interested organised groups, local authority and professional associations and the private sector, and as a result the local authorities are then left to implement these policies, often with considerable room for discretion, either for setting service standards or for local policy variations. As a result, the consequential delivery of services resulting from specific policies may be very different from that intended by those who made the policy initially. Housing, inner city programmes, regional policy all provide examples where policy intentions and policy consequences are ill matched, with the consequent re-appraisal of policy and the emergence of a new, nationally defined, policy.

This view is reinforced when the work of those who have studied the implementation and consequences of urban orientated policies is considered. Implementation studies bring out the complexities involved in service delivery; of co-ordinating the agencies involved, of securing agreement on what should be done and acquiring the resources to achieve policy goals; and above all the different perceptions and perspectives of the individuals and organisations involved. At the simplest level, this point is best made by the distinction between a top-down approach to implementation — the perspective as seen by central government and the national policy community — and the bottom-up approach — the perspective viewed from the agencies, local authorities and individuals concerned with policy implementation and service delivery on an areal or functional basis. The detailed knowledge of those in the locality, or the absence of precise advice from the centre, provides encouragement for those at the local level to develop different perspectives on policy issues from those at the centre, as the work of people like Levitt and Davies show.[25] Such work also shows how often policy implementation fails to be co-ordinated or monitored, especially by those who established the policy initially. In this sense, the myth that policy, once made, is implemented without any complications or implications for policy-makers, though often maintained in practice, is being destroyed by the academic and practical work done on policy implementation.

In part this work is supported by that which attempts to evaluate policy and its consequences and particularly that which seeks to understand both intended and unintended consequences of policy decisions. The distinction between intended and unintended policy consequences is an important one, referring to the extent to which policies successfully achieve what is expected of them as distinct to having a series of consequences which were never expected or intended. The consequences of virtually every policy decision are mixed. In housing, for example, it is doubtful whether either Labour governments concerned with giving tenants both security of tenure and some limitations on rents intended the size of the private rental sector to decline as rapidly as it has or that Conservatives concerned with improving the return to private landlords in 1956 intended this to result in the excesses of Rachmanism, whereby sitting tenants were severely harassed by landlords seeking to persuade them to leave their controlled tenancies, so that rents would become decontrolled (and could thus be increased) as a result. Virtually every policy field will produce simple unintended consequences such as those described here.

Apart from a concern with the intended and unintended consequences of policy, studies seeking to evaluate policy are also concerned with assessing who benefits and who loses from particular policy decisions. At present, this sort of work remains limited, and, in the British literature, is largely concerned with exploring class differences in terms of policy costs and benefits, though work in the race field is also concerned with the effects of policies in racial terms. Thus, Saunders, in his work on Croydon, shows how that authority's planning and land use policies have generally benefitted the commercial developers and home owning middle-class in the south of the borough, with few benefits going to the working class in the northern end of Croydon.

Though political scientists have been concerned with this work, again much of the main contribution has come from sociologists as well as geographers, both of whom have been particularly concerned with the spatial consequences of policy. Harvey's important contribution in 1973 is a landmark, subsequently followed by other contributions by urban political geographers both here and in the United States.[26] Writing predominantly from a Marxist and/or a managerialist perspective, such authors have demonstrated the inequities that exist on an areal basis in the distribution of public goods and services, though such contributors have also raised questions about the value of space, or geography, as an independent explanatory variable. In other words, whilst such writers highlight that different people and groups in the city have access to differing patterns of public goods and services, the explanation for this pattern of distribution is placed upon such variables as the operation of the market system or the activities of state agencies and *not* upon geographical variables *per se*.

This work on the distributional consequences of public policies and the provision of public goods — what might be called the outcomes of the system — is an important element in the growing literature concerned with policy evaluation. Such work tends to be of an interdisciplinary nature rather than the province of any particular one and is normally concerned with a particular policy arena or aspect of it. Hall's work on post-war British planning or that of Paris *et al.* on aspects of Birmingham's housing policy provide good examples.[27] Such work is indicative of the kind of development which is likely to be increasingly followed in the future, particularly as pressures on the social sciences to undertake 'relevant' research and teaching increase.

Central-Local Government Relations

The third major area of recent research and teaching interest is that of relations between central government and local authorities. Perhaps more properly called intergovernmental relations (following the North American style), the topic has seen a major research boost from the SSRC, whilst the activities of Mr. Heseltine at the DoE, as well as Scottish and other policy Ministers concerned with local authority services, have provided an almost daily initiative for teachers to absorb and pass on to their students. Whilst the 1980 Local Government, Land and Planning Act and its aftermath, together with current proposals for rate capping and rate referenda, are of central concern, other developments in education and housing are no less important. At the core of the practical and academic debates lies the issue of how far central government can and should control the activities of independently elected (and hence democratic) local authorities.

Until the mid-seventies, the relationship between central and local government was largely considered to be one in which local authorities were seen as either (albeit junior) partners or agents of central government, with the largely untested but predominant view being that local authorities had become little more than agents of the centre as a result of the increasingly centralised nature of British politics and government which had taken place during the twentieth century. Such a view was challenged by writers like Boaden and Stanyer,[28] who pointed to the wide variation in local authority services which exists, to the discretion which local authorities had in the performance of their duties, and the difficulty which central government had in imposing its will on particular local authorities. This last point was illustrated by such cases as Clay Cross and the 1972 Housing Finance Act (the authority refused to implement the rent increases imposed under the terms of the Act) and Tameside in 1977, when an attempt by the Secretary of State for Education to force the authority to modify their comprehensive education scheme was successfully defeated in the courts.[29]

However, it was the publication of the Layfield report on Local Government Finance in 1976 and of a CPRS paper on central-local government relations in 1977 which focused attention anew on the subject. Both highlighted the extent to which relations between central government and local authorities were complex, confused and ambiguous. Building on these reports, the SSRC established a Panel on central-local relations which, together with its successor, has produced a number of publications and established a major research programme.[30] The result of this initiative has been to change our conceptualisation of central-local government relations away from the agent-partner model to one based on inter-organisational analysis stressing ideas of resource dependency, bargaining and interdependence. The main exponent of this view is R. A. W. Rhodes, whose framework underpinned the initial Panel's report and research programme and who sees central government and local authorities as a set of mutually dependent organisations bargaining with each other in an attempt to increase their resources so as to pursue their goals and objectives more effectively. Therefore one can examine the resources (such as political, professional, legal or financial) which both central government and local authorities have at their disposal and the way in which these resources are used in the bargaining process which characterises the relationship between them. More recently, Rhodes has moved towards a more corporatist view of intergovernmental relations, stressing such concepts as the national community of local government and of policy community, and the corporatist nature of the bargaining process in which these communities are involved.

Using these ideas, the SSRC Panel established a number of research projects designed to examine the *processes* of central-local government relations and particularly the resource networks involved. Some of the research results are currently beginning to appear, but George Jones' edited book also gives some idea of what is involved.[31] In its subsequent programme, the Panel has focused on the central question of economic theory, the grant system and the impact of public sector unionisation on central-local relations, as well as developing projects to see how far relations between centre and locality vary between policy arenas and between different territories. In other words, central-local relations may vary because of differences in the nature of policy (housing as against transport) or because they are conducted within different territorial frameworks. For example, the existence of a Welsh or Scottish Office produces different patterns of central-local government relations in those countries as compared with England.

Much of this work is still in progress and some is only just beginning. All of it, of course, is being done amidst what all commentators would agree is the most important change in central-local relations in this century, one which will prove of considerable constitutional importance if carried to its logical extreme. Undoubtedly, Mr. Heseltine's legislation has altered the constitutional balance between centre and locality very much in favour of the centre, for whatever reasons. Heseltine's case rests on the primacy of central government policies (and especially macroeconomic expenditure policy) over those of local government, supplemented by a strong desire to penalise (particularly Labour controlled) overspending authorities. Proposals to limit the levels at which rates can be levied, after which the Minister would have the power to set the rate for the following financial year, would all limit severely local authorities' ability to *finance* their activities should they seek to deviate from what central government in the form of the DoE sees fit, however infrequently such a power might be used by the Minister. These proposals would further curtail local authority discretion, already severely limited by earlier legislation. Local government is thus in a vice which is constantly being tightened by central government in a fashion previously unknown in Britain, and the consequences of this policy would appear disastrous for the much vaunted independence of local authorities – which helps explain the opposition of both Labour and Conservative controlled local authority associations to these proposals.

Whatever the outcome of the present debate, local government in the eighties will be different from that of the seventies. It will no doubt find a new role and a new relationship with the centre, but undoubtedly this present period of change in the relationship between central and local government represents an exciting opportunity for the teacher of Urban Politics.

The Urban Fiscal Crisis

The last major area of interest currently drawing the attentions of researchers and teachers of Urban Politics concerns the extent to which urban government is in fiscal crisis, a theme which has attracted international attention and is not solely limited to Britain. Indeed most of the work on 'the fiscal crisis of local government' has been done on a comparative basis, with recent important contributions by Newton, Sharpe and Bahl.[32] Also part of this literature is that concerned specifically with local government finance, and the works of Layfield; Foster *et al.*, Travers and Burgess,[33] are all important here.

The easiest and most concise statement of the issues involved in the question of the urban fiscal crisis is to be found in Newton, K: *Balancing the Books.* In essence, local government finds itself in a resource squeeze both for demand and supply reasons. Better and bigger services; the introduction of new services; the replacement of social capital (housing, roads, sewers); increasing costs of service provision due to the labour intensive nature of local government and the combined effects of inflation and public sector unionisation are all causes of increased expenditure by local authorities. At the same time as expenditure has been rising, however, local authorities have been facing restrictions on their income, both in Britain and elsewhere. Local taxes, particularly the property based tax (the rates) in Britain lack buoyancy. Unlike national taxes, such as income and sales tax, income from local taxes fails generally to keep pace with inflation. Furthermore, taxes on property, such as the rates, are particularly visible from the taxpayers' point of view and have to be met out of net income, perhaps as a lump sum payment. Local taxes such as these are therefore politically sensitive in the extreme, with local politicians generally unwilling to introduce mammoth increases in tax rates to meet spiralling service costs. There have been a number of exceptions (mainly Labour authorities) in recent months, especially in the face of declining central government grants. These latter have been falling as a percentage of the total of local authority income in Britain since the mid-seventies, first as a result of the introduction of cash limits and second following on deliberate attempts to reduce the Exchequer contribution to local authorities as well as changes in the way in which grants are calculated.

Though other countries, such as Italy and America, face severe resource squeezes on urban authorities, the squeeze is particularly severe in urban Britain, partly because of the higher cost of urban services as compared with those provided by rural authorities. But the most significant factor in explaining the resource squeeze in Britain is the unbuoyant nature of the rates. Countries whose main local source of taxation is property appear more prone to resource squeezes than do countries whose local authorities have access to other forms of local tax revenue, and Britain is peculiarly dependent on a very limited property tax. This point is a central argument in Layfield and in other writings on British local government finance, highlighting the demand for the introduction of alternative sources of revenue. To date (Government Green Papers notwithstanding) central government has been reluctant to offer local authorities a significant bite at any of the more buoyant tax apples, and the call for the introduction of a local income tax continues to fall on deaf ears. The severity of the local fiscal crisis seems likely not only to continue, but also to increase, unless new resources are found or else considerable reductions in service levels made. This latter development is essentially implied by central government policy, which also encourages the privatisation of services where applicable. Such a strategy fits with the Conservative government's desire both to reduce the scope of the public sector and the level of public expenditure.

CONCLUSION

Issues such as those outlined above, as well as those discussed earlier under the themes of policy and central-local government relations are very much at the heart of current work in the field of Urban Politics. Though other topics, such as local level participation, the role of interest groups and the changing nature of local party politics and the media all attract attention, none of these have been anything like the centre of activity, even though they are not unimportant topics. Current concerns not only reflect both practical politics and the research interests of those concerned with the field, but are also linked to the wider concerns of Political Science as a whole. Thus we have already noted the links between Rhodes' work on the communities of local government, their intergovernmental relations and corporatist writings and theories. To this, we could add the growing body of Urban Politics literature which, though empirically located in local government, is theoretically located in Marxist writings. The Urban Politics literature is thus linked up, not only with other substantive parts of Political Science, such as Political Sociology, Comparative Studies, Policy Analysis or British Government and Politics, but also transcends the discipline's boundaries, and, as we have seen, forges links with other social sciences and with History in its efforts to understand the urban. It is the combination of this essentially interdisciplinary character, together with its practical, immediate relevance, and the theoretical possibilities offered which makes the study of urban politics one of the most exciting and rewarding fields for students of politics at present.

• NOTES

1. Literature treating these topics include W. D. Hawley and F. M. Wirt (eds.): The Search for Community Power (Englewood Cliffs: Prentice Hall, 1969), C. M. Bonjean, T. N. Clark and R. L. Lineberry (eds.): Community Politics (New York: Free Press, 1971); R. L. Lineberry and I. Sharkansky: Urban Politics and Public Policy (3rd Edition, New York: Harper and Row, 1978) and B. Hankins: Urban Politics and Policies (New York: Bobbs Merrill, 1972).

2. See for example P. Saunders: Urban Politics: a Sociological Interpretation (Harmondsworth: Penguin, 1980); M. Castells: The Urban Question (London: Edward Arnold, 1975) and City, Class and Power (London: Macmillan, 1979); R. A. Pahl: Whose City (Harmondsworth: Penguin, 1975) and J. M. Simmie: Power, Property and Corporatism (London: Macmillan, 1981).

3. See, for example, D. Harvey: Social Justice and the City (London: Edward Arnold, 1973); K. R. Cox (ed.): Urbanisation and Conflict in Market Societies (London: Methuen, 1978); D. T. Herbert and D. M. Smith (eds.): Social Problems and the City (Oxford: OUP, 1979) and A. D. Burnett and R. J. Taylor (eds.): Political Studies from Spatial Perspectives (Chichester: John Wiley, 1981).

4. Examples include E. P. Hennock: Fit and Proper Persons (London: Edward Arnold, 1973; D. Fraser: Urban Politics in Victorian England (Leicester: Leicester Univ. Press, 1976) and Power and Authority in the Victorian City (London: Macmillan, 1979); M. J. Daunton: Coal Metropolis: Cardiff 1870-1914 (Leicester: Leicester Univ. Press, 1977).

5. Urban Economics is a more specialised field, but see, for example, R. L. Lineberry (ed.): The Politics and Economics of Public Services (London: Sage, 1978); H. W. Richardson: Urban Economics (Harmondsworth: Penguin, 1973); W. Z. Hirsch: Urban Economic Analysis (New York: McGraw Hill, 1973) and W. K. Tabb and I. Sawers: Marxism and the Metropolis (Oxford: OUP, 1978).

6. J. G. Bulpitt: Party Politics in English Local Government (London: Longman, 1967); W. A. Hampton: Democracy and Community (Oxford: OUP, 1970); D. Hill: Participation in Local Affairs (London: Penguin, 1970); G. W. Jones: Borough Politics (London: Macmillan, 1969); J. M. Lee: Social Leaders and Public Persons (Oxford: OUP, 1976; P. Saunders, op. cit., J. Stanyer: County Government in England and Wales (London: RKP, 1967). See also J. Dearlove: The Politics of Policy in English Local Government (Cambridge: CUP, 1973).

7. An important exception is Saunders, op. cit. Some of the reasons why there are few such studies are explored in K. Newton, 'City Politics in Britain and the United States', Political Studies, Vol. 17 (1969).

8. See M. Goldsmith: Politics, Planning and the City (London: Hutchinson, 1980), especially 31-33.

9. J. G. Wilson (ed.): City Politics and Public Policy (New York: John Wiley, 1968), 2.

10. K. Young: Environmental Management in Local Politics, in D. Kavanagh and R. Rose (eds.): New Trends in British Politics (London: Sage, 1977); J. Stanyer: Understanding Local Government (London: Fontana, 1976 and J. Stewart: The Responsive Local Authority (London: Charles Knight, 1974).

11. See for example R. L. Lineberry and I. Sharkansky, op. cit. and D. R.

Morgan and S. A. Fitzpatrick: Urban Political Analysis (New York: Free Press, 1972). For more recent American developments see Hawley et al.: Theoretical Perspectives on Urban Politics (Englewood Cliffs: Prentice Hall, 1976).

12. N. Boaden: Urban Policy Making (London, CUP, 1971); J. Dearlove, op. cit. K. Young: 'Values in the Policy process', Policy and Politics, Vol. 5, (1977) and K. Young and J. Kramer: Strategy and Conflict in Metropolitan Housing (London: Heinemann, 1978).

13. Pahl, op. cit.

14. Harvey, op. cit.: Cox, op. cit. and Herbert and Smith, op. cit.

15. R. Pahl: 'Managers, technical experts, and the state' in M. Harloe (ed.): Captive Cities (London: John Wiley, 1977) 49-60.

16. P. Dunleavy: Urban Political Analysis (London: Macmillan, 1980).

17. Saunders, op. cit.

18. R. A. W. Rhodes: Control and Power in Central-Local Government Relations (Farnborough: Gower/SSRC, 1981), especially chapter 5; R. Flynn: The Local State and Capital: Aspects of incorporation in structure planning; P. Saunders and A. Cawson: Class, Corporatism and Interest Intermediation, Papers presented at BSA/PSA Political Sociology Conference, Sheffield, January 1981.

19. T. R. Dye: Politics, Economics and the Public (Chicago: Rand McNally, 1966); I. Sharkansky (ed.): Policy Analysis in Political Science (Chicago: Markham, 1970); R. Hofferbert: The Study of Public Policy (New York: Bobbs Merrill, 1974); T. R. Dye and V. Gray: The Determinants of Public Policy (Lexington: D. C. Heath, 1980).

20. For example, R. J. Nicholson and N. Topham: 'The Determinants of investment in housing by local authorities', Journal of the Royal Statistical Society, series A, Vol. 134 (1971) and 'Urban Road Provision in England and Wales', Policy and Politics, Vol. 4 (1976); and J. LeGrand and D. Winter: 'Towards an economic model of local government behaviour', Policy and Politics, Vol. 5 (1977).

21. J. W. Alt, 'Politics and Expenditure Models' in Policy and Politics, Vol. 5 (1977); N. Boaden, op. cit.; B. Davies: Social Needs and Resources in Local Services (London: Michael Joseph, 1968).

22. For now, see K. Newton and L. J. Sharpe: 'Local Output research: some reflections', Policy and Politics, Vol. 5 (1977) and K. Newton, 'Community Performance in Britain', Current Sociology, Vol. 22 (1976).

23. See for example, N. Boaden, op. cit., as well as the contributions by L. J. Sharpe, T. Hansen and C. Skovsgaard in K. Newton (ed.): Urban Political Economy (London: Frances Pinter, 1981).

24. Examples include S. Elkin: Politics and Land Use Planning (London: CUP, 1973); M. Harloe et al.: The Organisation of Housing (London: Heinemann, 1974); C. Paris and B. Blackaby: Not Much Improvement (London: Heinemann, 1979); Young and Kramer, op. cit.

25. R. Levitt: Implementing Public Policy (London: Croom Helm, 1980) and T. Davies: Manpower Policy and Economic Goals: the role of the Manpower Comission, Project Working Paper no. 2, Bristol, SAUS, 1980. On implementation generally see J. Pressman and A. Wildavsky: Implementation (California: California Univ. Press, 1973); E. Bardach: The Implementation Game (Boston:

78

MIT Press, 1977); M. Hill, Implementation, SSRC Panel Report on Central-Local Government Relations, Appendix 2 (1979).

26. See Harvey, op. cit.; S. Pinch in Herbert and Smith, op. cit. and his Patterns of local authority housing allocations in Greater London. IBG Transactions (n.s.) Vol. 3, 1978. See also R. L. Lineberry: Politics and Economics of Public Service and his Equality and Public Policy (London: Sage, 1977) as well as J. Levy, A. Meltsner and A. Wildavsky: Urban Outcomes (California: California Univ. Press, 1974).

27. P. Hall, et al.: The Containment of Urban England (London: Allen and Unwin, 1973); J. Lambert, C. Paris and B. Blackaby: Housing Policy and the State (London: Macmillan, 1978); and Paris and Blackaby, op. cit.

28. N. Boaden, op. cit.: J. Stanyer: Understanding Local Government (London: Fontana, 1976).

29. On the role of law in central-local government relations, see M. Elliott, 'The Role of Law in Central-Local Government Relations', London, SSRC (1981).

30. Important references in this field include: Report of the (Layfield) Committee of Enquiry into Local Government Finance, HMSO (1976) especially Appendix 6; CPRS: Relations between Central Government and Local Authorities, HMSO (1977). The pioneering study remains J. A. G. Griffith: Central Departments and Local Authorities (London: Allen and Unwin, 1966). More recently see SSRC Panel Report, Central-Local Government Relations, London SSRC (1979); G. W. Jones (ed.): New Directions in Central-Local Government Relations (Farnborough: Gower/SSRC, 1980) and R. A. W. Rhodes, op. cit.

31. Jones, op. cit.

32. K. Newton: Balancing the Books (London: Sage, 1980); L. J. Sharpe: The Local Fiscal Crisis in Western Europe: Myths and Realities (London: Sage, 1981). R. A. Bahl (ed.): Urban Government Finance (Beverley Hills: Sage, 1981).

33. Layfield, op. cit.: C. D. Foster, R. Jackman and C. Pearlman: Local Government Finance in a Unitary State (London: Allen and Unwin, 1980); and A. Travers and T. Burgess: Ten Billion Pounds (London: Grant McIntyre, 1980).

SELECT BIBLIOGRAPHY

P. Dunleavy: Urban Political Analysis (London: Macmillan, 1980).

M. Goldsmith: Politics, Planning and the City (London: Hutchinson, 1980).
P. Saunders: Urban Politics: a Sociological Interpretation (Harmondsworth: Penguin, 1980).
D. McKay and A. Cox: The Politics of Urban Change (London: Croom Helm, 1979).
R. A. W. Rhodes: Control and Power in Central-Local Government Relations (Farnborough: Gower/SSRC, 1981).
A. Travers and T. Burgess: Ten Billion Pounds (London: Grant McIntyre, 1980).
K. Newton: Balancing the Books (London: Sage, 1980).

Public Administration

David J. Wilson and Neville C. Woodhead

Misunderstandings about the nature of Public Administration abound. This is partly because the term can be used in at least three different ways. As Peter Fletcher observes "it can be used to denote:
1. The *activity* of public servants
2. The *structure* of executive government: that is the institutions and pattern of relationships through which the activity of public servants is carried on
3. The *study* of 1 and 2"[1]

At a very basic level there is confusion about precisely what we understand by the term "public sector". Far too many authors see Public Administration as concerned only with *part* of the public sector, namely central and local government. The authors of one recent text book, for example, provide such a working definition: "By Public Administration, then, we mean the machinery of central and local government, the process of implementing political decisions, and the body of people involved in that process".[2] To limit Public Administration simply to central and local government is to omit from analysis roughly half the public sector.

THE EXTENT OF THE PUBLIC SECTOR

The civil service accounts for less than 10% of total public employment in Britain (623,000 in 1984). Local government currently (1984) employs over 2 million people despite recent attempts to apply drastic pruning, but a large number of public servants work for agencies that receive the bulk of their finances from public funds or are directed by a board appointed under the authority of Parliament, like nationalised industries. In addition, then, to examining central and local government the student of Public Administration must focus on the vast range of hived off public agencies: health authorities, water authorities, quangos and the like. There are over seven million workers employed in the public sector: only half of these work in central and local government. All the organisations for which these seven million people work are characterised by a greater or lesser degree of public accountability for their actions although nearly half of all public employees are not directly accountable to elected public officials. Instead as indicated above, they work for bodies appointed by Ministers.

It is crucially important to recognise the diversity of the public sector. Public administrators are not *only* people who work in Whitehall departments or town halls. The very limited perspective which is all too often presented has done little to broaden the appeal of Public Administration. Its scope has been reflected, for example, at Leicester Polytechnic where in recent years Public Administration degree students on their placement year have been employed by a very wide range of authorities. The list of placements, reproduced below, illustrates the diversity of the public sector. As well as central government departments and local authorities students have been placed with:

Passenger Transport Executives	Atomic Energy Research
International Air Radio	Establishment, Harwell
British Road Services	The Sports Council
British Steel Corporation	Health Authorities
British Gas	National Youth Bureau
Water Authorities	University Administration

Given the extent and diversity of the public sector it is important to see Public Administration courses as opening up career opportunities in a wide range of areas *not* simply central and local government. There is a pressing need to move away from the traditionally narrow British perception of Public Administration as little more than a study of the organisation and processes of central government departments and local authorities.

THE NATURE OF PUBLIC ADMINISTRATION

In his book *Administration: The Word and the Science*[3] Andrew Dunsire reminds us of the complexities associated with the word "administration". Indeed, he argues that there are at least fifteen meanings of the word ranging from carrying out decisions to initiating policy. So while public administrators might, on the one hand, be the vehicles for *implementing* political decisions the administrators themselves might well have had an important voice in *formulating* the initial policy. Contrary to some basic textbooks, therefore, there is far more to Public Administration than simply "the process of implementing political decisions".[4] In theory it is perfectly possible to distinguish the "political" from the "administrative", but in practice it is difficult if not impossible. Such blurring of the edges between politics and administration, of course, raises fundamental questions about the "legitimate" role of public administrators (non elected officials) in a democratic society.

MacRae and Pitt argue that, "Public administrators deal with the activities of the state as compared with private administrators who are concerned with the goals of non-state organisation".[5] While it would be a mistake to exaggerate the distinctiveness of the public and private sectors it is clear that Public Administration is concerned with the purposes of society as a whole rather than specific groups within society. Private sector administration has a more restricted set of aims and tends to be constrained by a particularly economistic outlook. On the other hand "profitability" is a much more ambiguous or even redundant notion in the sphere of social welfare. It really is economic idealism to assess the "costs" of many social innovations; and "costs" or "profit" from these exercises would essentially be socio-political rather than economic. Yet many economists still maintain that a valid assessment of public sector efficiency can be undertaken with tools devised for private sector analysis.

STUDYING PUBLIC ADMINISTRATION

It is possible to argue that Public Administration is Britain has at last come of age. As the late W. A. Robson observed, the study of the subject "has travelled a long way during the past twenty-five years or so."[6] Years ago it was seen as a forgotten discipline, often little more attention being given to it than as a "subject option" on a politics degree, or perhaps, a vocational diploma course. Today, however, several polytechnics offer CNAA honours degree courses in Public Administration and many universities take the subject seriously not only at undergraduate level but also at Masters level. In addition, the last few years have seen the growth of sub-degree work in the area, largely under the aegis of the Business and Technician Education Council.

One irony is that despite the recent flowering of interest in the subject area, Public Administration is no newcomer to the academic world. It might be more correct to maintain that the subject has re-established its rightful place amongst the liberal arts and social sciences rather than grown up as the latest in a long line of non-traditional disciplines. One might (if pushed) trace its historical roots to the work of Hesiod and later Plato in ancient Athens. With the rise of industrialism in the West many centuries later these embers were re-kindled by social commentators such as Marx and Weber who were acutely aware of the integral role of administrative science in advanced industrial society. Nevertheless, no matter how distinguished its intellectual heritage, Public Administration as a subject of study in British academic life was the Cinderella relation of Politics and Business Study programmes during the vast increase of interest in the social sciences in the mid 1960s.

Interestingly, the Public Administration taught in higher education today bears little resemblance to the content of those occasional, marginal, optional course units of the 1960s. One could argue that Public Administration today is the one truly interdisciplinary social science. Unlike many social studies programmes it does not offer a multi-disciplinary approach which is frequently little more than an excuse for the juxta-position of several introductory course units with little attempt to relate the content of each to some academically and practically viable qualification. Rather, Public Administration courses draw from a wealth of intellectual sources and practical experience. They draw from Politics, History, Economics, Sociology, Psychology, on the one hand and from quantitative studies, business management and decision-making theory on the other.

There remains, however, one major tension in the teaching of Public Administration: are students receiving an education *about* public administration or a training *for* public administration? Education rather than training has been the norm for degree courses but there are indications that a move towards more "practical" degrees is imminent. In 1975 Andrew Dunsire argued[7] that existing Public Administration curricula could, without losing status or rigour, be made considerably more "vocational", orientated towards equipping the student with a number of saleable skills such as elementary operational research, payroll programming, social surveying, forms design, public relations, information science, work study. While some such options have been introduced in a number of degree courses the major "practical" input invariably remains the one year placement (supervised work experience). Nevertheless, as Dunsire observed in 1980 there is a need to ask what *academically* has been the role of supervised work experience?

How does it fit into the curriculum as a whole? Is it in practice the only "training" element there is? Is it even designed to equip the student with skills?[8] One possibility suggested by Dunsire is a "Knowledge-oriented" 3 year degree competing in the general social science market while 4 year degrees are made considerably more "vocational", skills-oriented, and competing in the professional market. Such graduates could well obtain exemptions from large parts of the examinations for the corresponding professional bodies.[9]

This education/training tension will not be easily resolved but already a number of Public Administration degree courses provide graduates with some exemptions from professional examinations. At Leicester Polytechnic, for example, graduates can gain exemptions from examinations of the Institute of Personnel Management, the Institute of Health Service Administrators, the Association of Certified Accountants, the Institute of Chartered Secretaries and Administrators, to name but a few. Nevertheless, the integration of theory and practice on Public Administration courses at all levels represents a major teaching challenge.[10]

PUBLIC ADMINISTRATION AND THE STATE

The broad focus of concern for students of Public Administration is the activity of the state. Since the middle of this century we have witnessed an unprecedented expansion of the role of the British state. "Government Departments alone are responsible for controlling a total public expenditure of £58,000 million. This accounts for 53% of the gross national product."[11] Not only has state expansion occurred in the field of social provision, the heart of the current political battle-ground, but also through state aid to industry, the co-ordinating and regulatory functions of the state and the economy, and the increasing tendency towards the legal codification of social relations. Despite the illusions of politicians homesick for the halcyon days of minimal social intervention, despite the pipe dreams of the more bullish political economists of the extreme right, if society and indeed our basic socio-economic organisation is to continue the role of the state *cannot* decline substantially.

As the state has expanded it has become increasingly clear that the needs of public sector administration are not identical to the needs of business management. In all societies administrative decisions on social and political planes are linked to the basic socio-economic structure of society. As such the need is now, and will be in the future, for the development of highly skilled administrators who have an appreciation of social forces and the political environment far beyond the ramparts of the singular profit motivated business enterprise. It is naive and simplistic to see Public Administration as "running a business in a political environment". Sadly, many politicians all too frequently appear to make this mistake.

ACADEMIC DEVELOPMENTS

By no means all the developments in Public Administration during the last ten years should be seen as emerging from the demand side of a labour equation constructed by employers. Alongside the trend towards the practical application of administrative techniques there has been substantial academic progress in a number of areas. Three such areas are: the development and rediscovery of the state as an object of political analysis; the increasing complexity of governmental decision-making and the consequent need for more precise tools of policy study and, thirdly, the need for decision theory to take account of the specific requirements of public sector organisations.

The first two points are closely related. Traditionally, the study of politics in Britain concentrated upon constitutional/institutional analysis which tended to see Politics as a descriptive science based upon fact, law and interpretation. Politics was seen as a practice defined by the limits of governmental institutions. Later, particularly influenced by American theoretical developments, the emphasis shifted to a concentration upon the interaction of groups within the institutional guidelines of government. The primary objects of political analysis were thus the participants, their demands and (where appropriate) consequent legislation. The role of the state was relegated to the edge of political analysis. Society was seen as being self-regulating to possibly an even greater extent than Adam Smith ever envisaged. The rise of pluralist and group theorists during the twentieth century centred the attention of Political Science upon the multiple cross pressures of groups in society, in David Truman's words, "the balance wheel is a going political system"[12] or, as Bentley expressed it, "the state is to the best of my knowledge and belief no factor in our investigation."[13]

The autonomy of political analysis as a whole was threatened by this approach and the reductionist theory of government which ensued placed great reliance upon non-political factors such as culture, and relegated from view the detailed investigation of the state and governing processes which represent the major political concerns of Public Administration. Whilst group theorists have supposed their interest groups operate in an uncharted environment, in reality throughout the twentieth century the role of groups within the political system has become more and more organised and charted along the divisions of the state. Not only have one-party states such as Cuba or China, and military dictatorships such as Brazil and Uruguay sought to integrate their interest structures into the state organisation, but in the West too (for example EEC and EFTA) we have seen a systematic divergence from the uncharted political state. Today the state plays an overt and increasingly important role in determining the access and functioning of groups in the policy process. It is perhaps strange that Marxist and neo-Marxist theories of the state have ignored the central contribution of policy studies to the understanding of the processes of state. It may well be that this has occurred because of the lack of short term chances for Marxist participation in central government, but it is perhaps surprising that where Marxists have penetrated governmental institutions at the local level, as in Italy, the question of the need for an understanding of the policy process does not appear to have arisen.

Parallel, and yet often completely ignored, Marxist and neo-Marxist theories of politics have increasingly centred upon the analysis of the state and state processes. The state, it is unfortunately true, is all too frequently seen as a strictly dependent variable. Nevertheless, the work of Antonio Gramsci,[14] and later Nicos Poulantzas[15] has shown the importance of the state and its organisations for understanding political structure. Whilst these particular approaches suffer from major epistemological failures their emphasis remains upon the state as the central objective of political analysis let alone an important strand of politics in practice.

The essential nature of the state could perhaps be encapsulated in the mapping of the outer limits of policy inputs. In theoretical terms the process of designation would be quite simple, but the empirical follow through, the actual flow chart of the policy process, except in the case of unduly restrictive and selective case studies, would be very difficult indeed. It could well have reached such a point that the technical minutiae of the policy process is so all embracing that the detailed understanding of the policy process required by the public administrator will remain illusive. Certainly even the description of the role and function of central government departments in the policy process is now extremely complex. Traditionally Political Science had been concerned with the empirical and institutional description of these segments of the organisation of government, and this was a non too complex matter. Within this framework equations could balance the regulatory and decision-making processes within a department. With the growth of administrative science that equation became much more complex; new theoretical constructions were attempted. One particularly British notion was that of contingency theory from the Institute of Local Government Studies at the University of Birmingham (INLOGOV). But no single administrative methodology could suffice. The art of the public administrator has become simultaneously both more integrative in the academic sense and more specialised in terms of the systems and techniques used for analysis.

PUBLIC ADMINISTRATION AND BUSINESS STUDIES

A useful contrast can be made at this point with what is seen by some as a similar academic differentiation, namely the emergence of Business Studies from Applied Economics and Accounting. The notion that the study of business constitutes an academic field is quite different from the notions that underpin the study of Public Administration. Management sciences in this country have never been academic leaders but have tended to rely on traditional inputs from separate academic disciplines. Whilst there might have been grounds in the early 1960s for assuming a parallel training for public administrators and business managers in which the public administrator required only nationally additional knowledge of the political system, the case can be made no longer.

Where Business Studies assumes a single paradigm for the resolution of its administrative policy problems, Public Administration is by contrast a multi-dimensional subject in which no single goal can be ascribed. Business Studies uses other distinct academic subject areas to inform the resolution of problems with a goal directed emphasis; Public Administration, on the other hand, integrates inputs from other disciplines into a new framework which both defines and attempts to resolve problems.

One current challenge, however, is common to both studying Business and Public Administration – that of microtechnology. In both these areas very profound organisational changes have occurred in the last five years — and indeed, the pace of change can be expected to increase. The availability of small, cheap, computer facilities — coupled with the ever widening scope of applications for business systems in office management (word processors, etc.), has changed the face of the modern office. For the public administrator, however, the change is not simply one of reduced clerical staffing, combined with new working routines. The introduction of new technology brings with it problems of a wider nature. These problems extend throughout the political domain, and include questions of privacy, data protection as well as communications, use and access, all of which pose great challenges for future study. For the administrator in the last decade of this century there will be little doubt that information technology and in particular its use and control, will mark out the core of his or her assignments.

WHAT OF THE FUTURE?

Writing in 1976 R. A. W. Rhodes observed that three aspects of British Public Administration were particularly noteworthy:
1. The attempt to evaluate and translate American theories, especially organisation theory, to the British context.
2. Developments in Organisational Sociology which, although they were pioneered in the private sector, were now being applied to the study of public bureaucracies and which do not build explicitly on American theoretical developments.
3. The continued, if attenuated, survival of the traditional social critic approach to the study of public bureaucracies.[16]

Yet despite the increased importance of Organisational Sociology in recent years there can never be an identifiable core of subjects present in every Public Administration course. As Rhodes notes, "The key criterion becomes internal consistency between the topics covered and not the individual topics themselves."[17] Public Administration is multi-disciplinary; it is not simply a more vocational "government" degree, or a study of central and local institutions of government. It is much more than this. How long such degree courses will remain *educational* rather than *training* experiences is a crucial question. There is little doubt that vocationally oriented courses are currently attractive for obvious career reasons. Perhaps in the final analysis market forces will shape the future of courses in Public Administration and the "training" element will, rightly or wrongly, assume far greater prominence.

88

1. Peter J. Fletcher, "Public Administration" in H. V. Wiseman (ed.): Political Science (London: Routledge & Kegan Paul, 1967), 53, 54.

2. J. D. Derbyshire with D. T. Patterson: An Introduction to Public Administration (London: McGraw Hill, 1979), 3.

3. A. Dunsire: Administration: The Word and the Science (London: Martin Robertson, 1973).

4. Derbyshire and Patterson, ibid.

5. S. MacRae and D. Pitt: Public Administration: an introduction (London: Pitman, 1980), 7.

6. W. A. Robson, "The Study of Public Administration Then and Now" Political Studies, Vol. XXIII (1975), 193-201.

7. A. Dunsire, "Public Administration in the Polytechnics: Aims and Philosophy", Public Administration Bulletin, No. 19 (Dec. 1975), 34-45.

8. A. Dunsire, "Public Administration in the Polytechnics: Inputs and Outputs", Discussion paper presented at CNAA conference on Supervised Work Experience, 29th October 1980.

9. Dunsire, ibid.

10. See D. J. Wilson and J. R. Greenwood, "The Integration of Theory and Practice" in Teaching Public Administration Vol. 1 No. 4, (May 1979), 4.

11. MacRae and Pitt, op.cit., 13.

12. D. Truman: The Governmental Process (New York: Knopf second edition, 1971), 514.

13. A. Bentley: The Process of Government (Chicago: University of Chicago Press, 1908), 263.

14. A. Gramsci: Selections from the Prison Notebooks (London: Lawrence & Wishart, 1971).

15. N. Poulantzas: Political Power and Social Classes (London: NLB, 1973).

16. R. A. W. Rhodes, "Current Developments in British Public Administration: Some Comparisons with America", Public Administration Bulletin, No. 22 (December 1976), 61.

17. Rhodes, ibid., 69.

SELECT BIBLIOGRAPHY

S. MacRae and D. Pitt: Public Administration: an introduction (London: Pitman, 1980).

J. D. Derbyshire and D. T. Patterson: An Introduction to Public Administration (London: McGraw-Hill, 1979).

R. A. W. Rhodes "Current Developments in British Public Administration: Some Comparisons with America", Public Administration Bulletin, No. 22, December 1976.

R. A. Chapman, "The P.A.C. and Teaching Public Administration in the 1970s", Public Administration Bulletin, No. 34 December 1980.

R. A. W. Rhodes: Public Administration and Policy Analysis (Farnborough: Saxon House, 1979).

R. Lewis and C. Himsworth: Teaching Public Administration in Further and Higher Education (London: JUC, 1979).

R. G. S. Brown and D. R. Steel: The Administrative Process in Britain (London: Methuen, 1979).

J. Stanyer and B. C. Smith: Administering Britain (London: Fontana, 1976).

A. Dunsire: Administration: The Word and the Science (London: Martin Robertson, 1973).

A. Dunsire, "Public Administration in the Polytechnics: Aims and Philosophy", Public Administration Bulletin, No. 19 December 1975.

A. N. Gladden: A History of Public Administration (London: Frank Cass, 1972).

J. R. Greenwood and D. J. Wilson: Public Administration in Britain (London: Allen and Unwin, 1984).

Modern Political Economy

Chris Goodrich

A little over a decade ago, a prominent American political scientist claimed that what we now refer to as the 'economic approach to politics' was the 'shape of political theory to come' — that it would, in time, emerge as the dominant framework for political analysis.[1] Whether or not that prediction was entirely accurate still remains to be seen. However, there can be little doubt that since then, considerable progress has been made towards this goal. The use of methods and concepts derived from economics is now widely recognised as a significant innovation in the study of politics, and has gained a growing acceptance within the discipline while other, less robust approaches have fallen from favour.

In volume eight of *Teaching Politics,* Jeffrey Stanyer provided a useful introduction to this body of research.[2] Stressing the theoretical nature of its contribution, he outlined ways in which the economic approach has been applied to a variety of questions at both the positive and normative levels, accompanying this with a summary of, and proposed teaching programme based upon, the seminal works of Olson and Downs.[3] Extending and elaborating upon this theme, I shall, in this article, try to describe what we mean when we speak of the 'economic approach to politics'. In so doing, I shall argue that it provides us with a link between the economic and the political in terms of both the method employed and subject-matter dealt with. In the light of this argument, I shall go on to consider one of the most important new developments in this field since the publication of Down's *Economic Theory of Democracy* over two decades ago. Known as politico-economics or politico-econometrics, this application of the 'economic approach' has virtues other than novelty to recommend it in the context of our present discussion. On the one hand, it clearly illustrates the interdispliniary nature of this general body of research through its use of economic tools to investigate the interrelationship between the economy and polity. On the other, it has, as a Positive programme, been concerned not only with the *generation* of testable propositions, but also their *empirical testing,* using advanced econometric techniques.

By so doing, it can be said to have successfully combined what Stanyer has, perhaps inaccurately, called the theoretical and statistical modes of explanation.

THE ECONOMIC APPROACH TO POLITICS

Let us begin by considering what we mean by the 'economic approach to politics'. Like many other recent innovations in political analysis, the 'economic approach' consists of an intellectual framework, initially developed in the context of another discipline, which has subsequently been employed in the study of politics. The usual process by which this has occurred has been one in which political scientists have 'borrowed', or imported outside ideas, and have adapted them to their own purposes, applying them to problems of their own choosing. What distinguishes the 'economic approach' from the others is the fact that its primary impetus came not from within Political Science, but from an aggressive incursion on the part of economists into the political sphere. This movement has been cynically, though rather accurately described by Hirschman as one in which;

> .... economists have claimed that concepts developed for the purpose of analysing phenomena of scarcity and resource allocation can be success-fully used for explaining political phenomena as diverse as power, democracy, and nationalism. They have thus succeeded in occupying large portions of the neighbouring discipline while political scientists — whose inferiority complex vis-a-vis the tool-rich economist is equalled only by that of the economist vis-a-vis the physicist — have shown themselves quite eager to be colonised and have often actively joined the invaders.[4]

Having first been developed by economists and latterly taken up by political scientists, the 'economic approach to politics' has, over time, come to reflect the preoccupations of each. At the same time, interpretations of the nature of this development and the goals towards which it is directed have come to depend largely upon the disciplinary backgrounds and interests of those involved. To fully untangle the ideas involved would entail an extended diversion into the recent, and not so recent histories of economic and political thought.[5] At the heart of the matter however, we may identify essentially two major schools of thought, each concerned with a different set of problems which, when combined, form the basis of the economic approach.

(a) Economic Politics

The first, and perhaps most straightforward of these has been primarily concerned with economics as a mode of analysis, and its applicability to the political sphere. Within economics, this movement had its origins in something which Tullock has called 'Economic Imperialism'; a process by which economists, prompted by a belief in the generality and power of their analytic tools, have sought to extend them to areas other than that conventionally dealt with by the discipline.[6] Politics constitutes but one of a number of areas to which this exercise has been applied, among the more outlandish of which we may include sex, marriage, and the behaviour of the coal-tit.[7] Throughout however, the primary goal has been an examination of the extent to which any kind of behaviour or situation may fruitfully be seen in economic terms — in much the same way as we would test the usefulness of a spanner by the number of nuts and bolts it fitted.

Where it has concerned itself with the study of politics, Economic Imperialism has been complemented by the activity of a number of political scientists sharing a similar preoccupation with questions of method. Motivated by the desire to construct a 'science of politics', they see in economic analysis the possible basis of such an enterprise and, like the 'imperialists', have sought to explore ways in which notions such as rational choice, game and bargaining theory may be applied to political questions. For different reasons, both economists and political scientists have been engaged in the extension of methods and concepts derived from economics to the political. Summarising both movements, we may say that they have been directed towards the political application of economic analysis — what we shall call Economic Politics.

(b) Modern Political Economy

Although Economic Politics is a major component of the 'economic approach to politics', the two are not completely identical. Overlapping the former, is a second, and rather more complex body of research which seeks to operate along that ill-defined and underexplored boundary between the subject-matter of the economist and the political scientist. The distinction between the two is at best an artificial and somewhat arbitrary one, which has become increasingly blurred in modern societies. There are many areas of activity which are both economic and political in character and/or where the one exerts a profound influence upon the other. This line of enquiry is concerned with those areas where the economic and the political overlap, and employs Economic Politics as a means of approaching them. For this reason, it has come to be known as Modern Political Economy.[8]

The starting point for much of this research is to be found in a conception of society, and social institutions as mechanisms for satisfying individual wants in a world of scarce resources. Within economics, this has given rise to the problem of constructing a means of evaluating, and making decisions upon, the allocation and distribution of resources within society; what economists call a Social Welfare Function (S.W.F.).[9] Traditionally, economists have focused attention upon the market as a desirable want-satisfying mechanism. However, its distributional outcomes are frequently less than acceptable and, in the presence of imperfect information and markets, public goods and other externalities, it is unable to efficiently perform its allocative function. The S.W.F. is seen as a basis upon which an outside agency — usually government — is to act so as to remedy these shortfallings. Similarly, in socialist economics, the S.W.F. is put forward as a guide for the actions of a central planning agency, where the latter substitutes for the market entirely.[10] In essence, the construction of a Social Welfare Function may be regarded as the search for a means of making political decisions in an economic context, upon questions which are both political and economic in character. Leading proponents of this exercise have claimed that the problem may be generalised to one of what they call Social or Collective Choice.[11] Social Choice theory is concerned with finding a procedure or rule which satisfies a number of plausible conditions, capable of resolving individual preferences over alternative social states into a social preference or ordering. Perhaps the best known examples of the by now vast and often highly technical literature on this subject are the works of Arrow and Sen. Arrow showed that there is no such procedure or rule which is simultaneously consistent (or rational) and non-dictatorial in character.[12] Operating along much the same lines, Sen has pointed to a similar conflict between Liberalism and the Pareto-principle.[13]

Complementing the rather arid logical manipulations of the Social Choice theorist has been an examination of the rules or principles by which we ought to govern social activity undertaken by philosophers within a broadly contractarian framework.[14] Of these, the most famous is John Rawls' *A Theory of Justice*, where it was argued that rational individuals, operating behind a hypothetical, pre-contractual 'veil of ignorance' would choose two basic principles to be applied in any post-contractual state.[15] They are that; (a) each person is to have an equal right to the most extensive basic liberty compatible with a similar liberty for others and (b) social and economic inequalities are to be arranged so that they are both (i) reasonably expected to be to everyone's advantage, and (ii) attached to positions and offices open to all. Approaching this theme from a slightly different perspective, Nozick has tackled the problem of why individuals should wish to move from a pre-contractual state of anarchy to post-contractual society.[16] From there, he proceeds to an examination of normative arguments relating to the role of the state in an effort to justify a Libertarian society governed by what he calls the 'minimal State'..

Perhaps the most elaborate investigation of the institutional structure of society in general, and of the relationship between the economic and the political in particular, has been undertaken by members of the 'Public Choice' school and their associates. Their prolific work in this area has been motivated by a number of considerations, many of them rooted in economic theory, but which are of obvious relevance to the political analyst.[17] Broadly speaking we may say that the most important of these are:

(i) An aggressive Positivism which rejects the inclusion of Normative principles.

(ii) A recognition of the importance of the State in modern societies, and a desire to examine the basis of its existence and the role it plays with respect to the satisfaction of individual wants.

(iii) A rejection of the 'market failure' criterion for government intervention on the grounds that it is too simpliste; and the search for an alternative. At the heart of this is the notion that political, market, and other non-market forms of decision-making are all subject to 'failure' in that they have costs, as well as benefits associated with them. This, in turn, has given rise to an examination of the costs and benefits of different modes of decision-making – and the argument that the choice between them at any given time should depend upon their relative net benefits.

(iv) A rejection of the idea of a S.W.F. on the grounds that it assumes an unusual altruism on the part of those who are to implement it – this being inconsistent with the normal behavioural postulates of economic theory. Further, it provides an unreal picture of how political decisions are taken in the real world – ignoring the influence of political institutions entirely. In an attempt to make good these shortfallings, a number of Public Choice analysts have tried, wholly or in part, to construct models of the political process, based upon the notion that those involved act as rational, and relatively self-interested agents.

Two of the most outstanding contributions made by Public Choice theory have been in the areas of constitutional design and the creation of a positive theory of political behaviour.

In the first, James Buchanan, Gordon Tullock and others have sought to examine the way rational individuals would choose to arrange the institutional structure of society as a means of satisfying their wants in a contractarian context.[18] Starting from a Hobbesian analysis of anarchy, in which the latter is represented as a 'Prisoners' Dilemma' game (or rather, Super-game), they argue that individuals will eventually arrive at a pre-contractual equilibrium of violence, and thence the societal alternative in which each individual is assigned property rights, both in himself and in the resources at his disposal.[19] In this, the state is seen as having two major roles. As a 'protective agency', its function is to protect and enforce these property rights, as well as contracts made on the basis of them; thus preventing a reversion to anarchy, and facilitating mutually beneficial voluntary interaction, both in the market and elsewhere. As a 'productive' institution, it is seen as one among a number of mechanisms within society established for the satisfaction of individual wants through the supply of goods and services. Given this, it is argued that a society of rational individuals will establish a constitutional structure determining the scope, size and organisation of political institutions based upon the costs and benefits associated with each — and their magnitude relative to those deriving from other mechanisms.[20]

Closely related to the design of political institutions is the problem of determining how they operate in the real world. In an attempt to tackle this question, Public Choice theorists have sought to construct partial or complete models of the political process capable of generating empirically testable propositions. Among the latter, we may include the work of Buchanan and Tullock, concerned primarily with the behaviour of direct democracies, and that of Bartlett, Breton and Downs dealing with representative systems.[21] All are based upon the idea of government as a 'productive' agency in the broadest sense, and upon the existence of a circular relationship between government and governed of the kind outlined in Figure 1. Here, government produces a stream of costs and benefits in the form of goods, services, taxes, etc., which are consumed by members of society. The actual or expected stream of benefits and costs faced by an individual will, in turn, influence the demands or wants he feeds into the political process, whether through voting or some other form of behaviour.

96

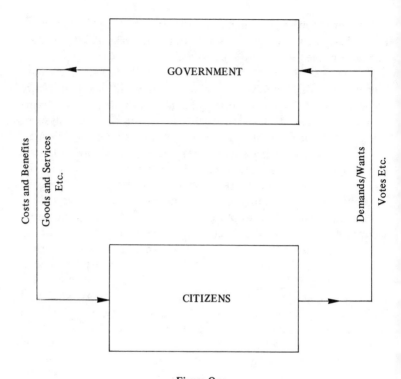

Figure One

**The Circular Relationship Between
Government and Governed**

Almost all of the advanced industrial democracies of the West are representative ones; making those models dealing with this kind of system particularly interesting. Of these, the best known is that developed by Downs. There, the political process is seen in terms analogous to the operation of the market. Rational politicians (or rather, political parties), motivated by the desire to gain or retain power, act as 'political entrepreneurs', competing with one another to 'sell' policies (i.e. bundles of costs and benefits) to the electorate in return for their vote. At the same time, the latter act in much the same way as they would in private market transations; 'spending' their vote on the party yielding the highest expected net benefits. Thus, other things being equal, the re-election constraint is seen as forcing vote-seeking politicans to act in conformity with the wishes of at least the majority of the electorate.[22] Other things are not usually equal however, and Bartlett, Breton and Downs all recognise that other factors, such as costly and imperfect information, participation costs, the distribution of power, the behaviour of interest and pressure groups, as well as that of the government bureaucracy can — and will — distort the outcome. Bartlett, for example, focuses attention upon the degree to which informational factors determine the distribution and exercise of power in a democracy. Breton, on the other hand, emphasises the extent to which policies are dependent upon the relative power of politicians and bureaucrats.[23]

POLITICO-ECONOMICS

The economic models of democracy put foward by Bartlett *et al.* have two major characteristics in common. First, although they represent an important approach to the political process *per se,* they were primarily developed for the purpose of examining the relationship between the economic and the political. Arguments as to the proper role of the state aside, there can be little doubt that in the advanced industrial economies of the world, government is the single most important determinant of economic activity; both as a regulator and as a producer/consumer of goods and services. Yet, until the advent of these models, economists had no theory of political behaviour commensurate with that of the market. Government was assumed to be exogenous to the system, and its actions were assumed to be that of a 'benevolent dictator', operating in the public interest.[24] Implicitly or otherwise, these new models have sought to endogenise political action into a general equilibrium system based upon the interaction between the economy and polity: showing how policies generated by self-interested politicans influence economic activity, how this in turn acts upon the consumer/voter, and thence feeds back into the political process. This scheme is outlined in Figure 2. The dotted line represents policies which are 'non-economic' in character, but which form part of the stream of costs and benefits 'consumed' by the electorate. The second characteristic is, of course, their 'positive' nature. Normative considerations are excluded, so far as is possible, the purpose of the models being seen as; providing an *explanation* of the behaviour of the actors involved, and generating testable *predictions* concerning their future activity under a given set of circumstances. Under the positivist rubric,

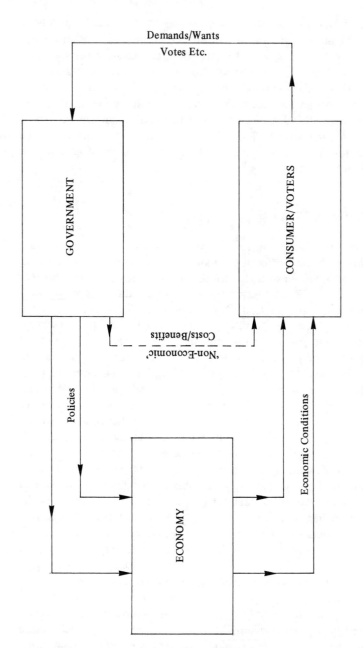

Figure Two

The Interaction Between Economy and Polity

the latter constitutes the most important test of a theory. Without prediction and testability, the explanatory power of a theory amounts to little more than plausible rationalisation, having much the same scientific status as an argument over the number of angels able to stand on a pin-head.

Together they form the basis for one of the newest developments in Modern Political Economy; Politico-Economics. In a sense, politico-economics may be regarded as an extension of the economic models of democracy dealt with above. Going somewhat further however, it is *explicitly* concerned with the interaction between economy and polity; formally modelling these relationships with the aid of economic analysis, *and* subjecting them to empirical test using sophisticated statistical techniques.

Up until now, politico-economists have focused attention upon a simple system of the kind shown in Figure 3. Here, the electorate are seen as rational agents, their support for the government of the day depending upon the state of the economy. The incumbent party (or parties) is equally rational, seeking, amongst other things, to retain power.[25] Because it is aware (or believes in the existence) of a relationship between economic conditions and political support, it will use the policy instruments at its disposal to manipulate the economy in an effort to win the next election.

The outcome of this interaction may differ considerably from the desirable one postulated by Downs and his followers. Representing the economy by two variables; inflation and unemployment, theorists such as Nordhaus and MacRae have shown that government vote-seeking policies can have entirely unacceptable consequences.[26] In the long-run, they generate higher rates of inflation than are socially optimal, whilst in the short-run they promote a government induced destabilisation of the economy over the electoral term; what has come to be known as the *Political Business Cycle*. Underlying the latter is the idea that, in the run-up to an election, a government will boost the economy, hence reducing unemployment and increasing income, in an effort to gain votes. Where correctly managed, the inflationary consequences of this action will not feed through the economy until after the election. By then however, the government will have initiated strongly deflationary policies, so as to 'invest' for the next pre-election period.

There is now considerable evidence to suggest both that economic conditions influence political support and that government economic policy is motivated by the desire to win votes. Studies of government

100

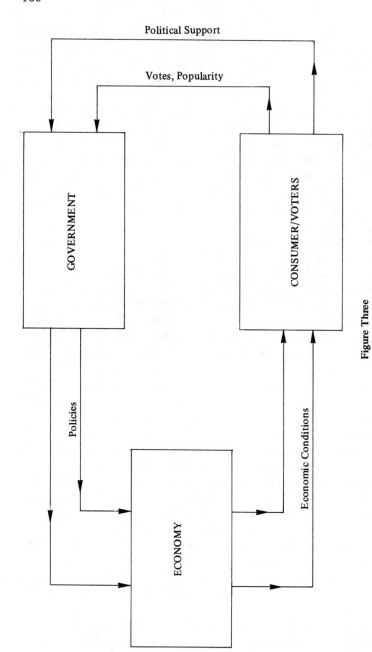

Figure Three
The Basic Politico-Economic Model

popularity and voting behaviour for the U.S., U.K., France, W.Germany and elsewhere indicate that both are influenced to a significant extent by factors such as inflation, unemployment, and movements in real and nominal income.[27] Similarly, observers such as Nordhaus, Tufte, Ben-Porath and Averch *et al.* have gathered considerable *prima facie* evidence that the economies of a large number of states exhibit electorally related cyclical movements.[28]

Most impressive of all however, have been the econometrically based studies of the simultaneous interaction of voter and government behaviour undertaken by Frey, Schneider and other members of the so-called 'Zurich School'. Going beyond the simple vote-seeking model, they argue that governments will also seek to pursue their own ideological goals; e.g. Left-wing administrations will display a preference for low unemployment, whilst those of the Right will prefer price stability.[29] The trade-off between the two is seen as being determined by the incumbent's current standing with the electorate (as given by its popularity), and the proximity of the next election. The influence of bureaucracy and additional constraints such as the need to maintain a 'respectable' balance of payments position are also introduced. Frey *et al.* then examine the influence of these factors on the use of *policy instruments*, and thence upon the economy. From there, they close the circle by dealing with the impact of the economy on government popularity. The theoretical sophistication of this model is matched only by the degree to which it is able to explain the post-war politico-economic experience of the U.S., U.K., and W. Germany. Its power from the economic standpoint alone may be judged by the fact that for W.Germany, it was consistently able to outperform the statistical model of the economy employed by the Federal government![30]

The simplicity, and apparent fruitfulness of this basic framework invite extensions to other areas of potential interest to both the economist and political scientist. We may introduce other actors into the system, showing how, for example, the behaviour of big business and trade unions influence and is in turn influenced by, politico-economic interaction. On the other hand, we might wish to examine the relationships already dealt with in greater detail. What is the link between economic and political stability, and what are the long-term consequences for political and economic institutions of these short-term relationships? Normative questions arising from the politico-economist's findings might also be considered. Democracy and economic stability are both seen as desirable — yet it would appear that the two are, at least in some circumstances, incompatible. Which of the two are to predominate, or is it possible to discover some means of overcoming the problem without sacrificing either?

CONCLUSION

In his paper, Jeffrey Stanyer tried to show how the deductive approach in general, and the economic approach in particular provided a powerful basis for theoretical political analysis capable of resolving differences between modern and traditional ways of thinking about the subject. Going somewhat further, I have tried to achieve two goals. Firstly, to demonstrate that the 'economic approach' has an empirical as well as a theoretical contribution to make to the study of politics. Secondly, to show how it provides a link between economics and politics, not only in terms of the method employed − but also with respect to the problems dealt with, problems which lie at the very heart of our understanding of modern society. By so doing, it has brought us at least part of the way from the discipliniary insularity so pungently criticised by Ross when he wrote;

> .... today it must be seriously doubted whether there is any such thing as a purely economic activity, purely political activity or even purely religious activity. ... If different aspects of social behaviour have now become integrated, does it not follow that the separate disciplines of social study must be brought together correspondingly? Otherwise we have partial sciences, compared by Ruskin to a science of gymnastics which assumed that men had no skeletons.[31]

● NOTES

1. W. Mitchell, 'The Shape of Political Theory to Come', American Behavioural Scientist, Volume 11 (1967), 8-20/37.

2. J. Stanyer, 'The Deductive Approach in the Study of Politics', Teaching Politics, Volume 8 (1979), 171-182.

3. M. Olson: The Logic of Collective Action (Cambridge Mass.: Harvard University Press, 1971) A. Downs: An Economic Theory of Democracy (N.Y.: Harper & Row, 1957).

4. A. Hirschman: Exit, Voice and Loyalty (Cambridge Mass.: Harvard University Press, 1970), 19.

5. For a taste of this background, the reader should consult J. Buchanan and

G. Tullock: The Calculus of Consent (Ann Arbor: University of Michigan Press, 1965), Appendices I & II.

6. G. Tullock, 'Economic Imperialism' in J. Buchanan and R. Tollison (eds.): Theory of Public Choice (Ann Arbor: University of Michigan Press, 1972), 317-329.

7. G. Tullock, 'The Coal-Tit as a Careful Shopper', The American Naturalist, Number 105 (1971), 77-80. R. McKenzie and G. Tullock: The New World of Economics (Homewood Ill.: Irwin, 1978).

8. For a dissenting view on the use of this term see W. Letwin: On the Study of Public Policy (London: L.S.E., 1979). For an economist's approach to the need for an analysis of the overlap between the economic and the political see J. Buchanan, 'Toward Analysis of Closed Behavioural Systems' in Buchanan and Tollison (eds.), op. cit. 11-23.

9. See A. Bergson, 'A Reformulation of Certain Aspects of Welfare Economics', Quarterly Journal of Economics, Volume 52 (1938), 310-334 and P. Samuelson: Foundations of Economic Analysis (N.Y.: Atheneum, 1974), Ch.8. For a readable introduction to this and most other questions associated with the development of Modern Political Economy see C. Rowley and A. Peacock: Welfare Economics: A Liberal Restatement (London: Martin Robertson, 1975).

10. See W. Brus: The Economics and Politics of Socialism (London: Routledge and Kegan Paul, 1973), Ch.5.

11. See K. Arrow: Social Choice and Individual Values (New Haven N.J.: Yale University Press, 1963), Cowles Foundation Monograph No.12. A. Sen: Collective Choice and Social Welfare (London: Oliver and Boyd, 1970). See also D. J. Mayston: The Idea of Social Choice (London: Macmillan, 1974).

12. Arrow, op. cit.

13. A. Sen, 'The Impossibility of a Paretian Liberal', Journal of Political Economy, Volume 78 (1970), 152-157. For an extensive survey of the literature on this problem see A. Sen, 'Liberty, Unanimity and Rights', Economica, Volume 43 (1976), 217-245.

14. For a discussion of the major contributions see S. Gordon, 'The New Contractarians', Journal of Political Economy, Volume 84 (1976), 573-590.

15. J. Rawls: A Theory of Justice (Cambridge Mass.: Harvard University Press, 1971).

16. R. Nozick: Anarchy, State and Utopia (Oxford: Basil Blackwell, 1974).

17. For a useful introduction to these questions see J. Buchanan, 'Public Finance and Public Choice', National Tax Journal, Volume 28 (1975), 384-394.

18. Buchanan and Tullock, op. cit. and J. Buchanan: The Limits of Liberty (Chicago: University of Chicago Press, 1975).

19. For general discussions of anarchy from the economic point of view see G. Tullock (ed.): Explorations in the Theory of Anarchy (Blacksburg Va.: Center for Study of Public Choice, 1972) and G. Tullock (ed.): Further Explorations in the Theory of Anarchy (Blacksburg Va.: University Publications, 1974). For an excellent mathematical treatment of anarchy and the argument for the State see M. Taylor: Anarchy and Co-operation (London: Wiley, 1976). An introduction to the notion of property rights is given in E. Furubotn and S. Pejovich (eds.): The Economics of Property Rights (Cambridge Mass.: Ballinger, 1974).

104

20. Buchanan and Tullock, op. cit. An excellent critique of this approach is given in B. Barry: Political Argument (London: Routledge and Kegan Paul, 1965), 237-285.

21. Buchanan and Tullock, op. cit. Downs, op. cit. R. Bartlett: Economic Foundations of Political Power (N.Y.: The Free Press, 1973) and A. Breton: The Economic Theory of Representative Government (London: Macmillan, 1974).

22. For a dissenting view, and an extended discussion of individual choice in the market and the political sphere see J. Buchanan, 'Social Choice, Democracy and Free Markets', Journal of Political Economy, Volume 62 (1954), 114-122 and J. Buchanan, 'Individual Choice in Voting and the Market', Journal of Political Economy, Volume 62 (1954), 334-343.

23. Breton, op. cit. There now exists an extensive sub-literature on the behaviour of bureaucracy, for a flavour of these contributions see T. Borcherding (ed.): Budgets and Bureaucrats – The Sources of Government Growth (Duke University Press, 1977).

24. A point consistently emphasised in the writings of James Buchanan and other members of the Public Choice School. For a discussion of conventional economic theories, or rather, non-theories of government behaviour see Downs, op. cit. Chs.1 & 15.

25. Good surveys of the literature in this field are to be found in B. Frey and F. Schneider, 'On the Modelling of Politico-Economic Interdependence' European Journal of Political Research, Volume 3 (1975), 339-336 and B. Frey, 'Politico-Economic Models and Cycles' Journal of Public Economics, Volume 9 (1978), 203-220.

26. W. Nordhaus, 'The Political Business Cycle', Review of Economic Studies, Volume 42 (1975), 169-190. D. MacRae, 'A Political Model of the Business Cycle', Journal of Political Economy, Volume 85 (1977), 239-263.

27. The literature on this question is enormous. For representative work see G. Kramer, 'Short Term Fluctuations in U.S. Voting Behaviour 1896-1964', American Political Science Review, Volume 65 (1971), 131-143. C. Goodhart and R. Bhansali, 'Political Economy', Political Studies, Volume 18 (1970), 43-106. J. Lafay, 'The Impact of Economic Variables on Political Behaviour in France' mimeo University of Poitiers (1978) G. Kirchgassner, 'Oekonometrische Schatzungen des Einflusses der Wirtschaftslage auf die Popularitat der Parteien', Schweizerische Zeitschrift fur Volkswirtschaft und Statistik, Volume 110 (1974), 409-445.

28. Nordhaus, art. cit. E. Tufte: Political Control of the Economy (Princeton: Princeton University Press, 1978) Y. Ben-Porath, 'The Years of Plenty and the Years of Famine: A Political Business Cycle', Kyklos, Volume 28 (1975), 400-403. H. Averch, J. Koehler and F. Denton: The Matrix of Policy in the Phillipines (Princeton: Princeton University Press, 1971).

29. For a theoretical formulation see B. Frey and L. Lau, 'Towards a Mathematical Model of Government Behaviour', Zeitschrift fur Nationalokonomie, Volume 28 (1968), 355-380 and 'Ideology, Public Approval and Government Behaviour', Public Choice, Volume 10 (1971), 20-40. For independent evidence on this count see D. Hibbs, 'Political Parties and Macroeconomic Policy', American Political Science Review, Volume 71 (1977), 1467-1487. Work by Hibbs and Schneider also appears to indicate that public attitudes towards

variables such as unemployment and inflation are determined in some degree by their socio-economic position see D. Hibbs, 'The Mass Public and Macroeconomic Performance: the dynamics of public opinion towards unemployment and inflation', American Journal of Political Science (23) 1979, 705-731 and F. Schneider, 'Different (Income) Classes and Presidential Popularity: An Empirical Analysis', Munich Social Science Review, Volume (1978/2), 53-69.

30. B. Frey and F. Schneider, 'A Politico-Economic Model of the United Kingdom', Economic Journal, Volume 88 (1978), 243-253. B. Frey and F. Schneider, 'An Empirical Study of Politico-Economic Interaction in the United States', Review of Economics and Statistics, Volume 60 (1978), 174-183. B. Frey and F. Schneider, 'An Econometric Model with an Endogenous Government Sector', Public Choice (23) 1979, 29-43.

31. A. Ross: Trade Union Wage Policy (Berkeley: University of California Press, 1950), 7.

SELECT BIBLIOGRAPHY

The number of works now published dealing with both the 'Economics of Politics' and Modern Political Economy is horrifically large. Useful introductions to both the literature and the major issues dealt with are to be found in the works given below. Those suitable for use on an introductory course are marked with an asterisk.

J. Alt: The Politics of Economic Decline (Cambridge: Cambridge University Press, 1979).

J. Alt and K. A. Chrystal: Political Economics (London: Wheatsheaf Books, 1983).*

R. Amacher et al.: The Economic Approach to Public Policy (Cornell: Cornell University Press, 1976).

B. Frey: Modern Political Economy (Oxford: Martin Robertson, 1978).*

D. A. Hibbs and H. Fassbinder (eds.): Contemporary Political Economy (London: North-Holland, 1981).

Institute of Economic Affairs: The Economics of Politics, IEA Readings No. 18 (London: IEA, 1978).

D. Mueller: Public Choice (Cambridge: Cambridge University Press, 1979).

W. Riker and P. C. Ordeshook: An Introduction to Positive Political Theory (Englewood Cliffs: Prentice-Hall, 1973).

G. Tullock: The Vote Motive (London: IEA, 1976).*

P. Whiteley (ed.): Models of Political Economy (London: Sage, 1980).

International Relations

Steve Smith

One of the major problems in the study of International Relations has been, and remains, that of deciding what its subject-area is. Of course, there have been many debates over methodology, mirroring in large part the divisions in the subject of Political Science generally, but International Relations has, since its development as a separate subject following the end of the First World War, been continually concerned with the question of what are the main features for study. At no time has this debate been more fundamental than at the present: since the Soviet intervention in Afghanistan in December 1979 the discipline has been faced with a kind of identity crisis. Whereas twenty years ago the focus of enquiry seemed obvious, in that International Relations was clearly concerned with security, and specifically the East-West split in the international system, and whereas ten years ago there was widespread agreement that the focus was economic, specifically the North-South split, the current position is far less clear. Of course, it must be pointed out that neither of these positions was accepted by all those who studied the subject, although it was clear that each, in its own way, constituted a paradigm. Nevertheless, the problems concerning the present period seem far more serious. For what has happened is that the clock seems to have shifted back and the traditional concerns of the subject-area now seem once again to be relevant: the present international political system has many features that seem to be in sharp contrast to those that characterised it from the late 1960s onwards. The current downturn in US-Soviet relations, as witnessed by the breakdown of arms control and the crisis over the deployment of Cruise and Pershing II missiles in Europe in late 1983, seems to have more in common with the 1950s than with the 1970s. Yet at the same time as the world is concerned with security issues, economic pressures and the effects of interdependence seem to be of continued and significant importance.

In essence, the problem is that in the 1970s the international political system seemed to be in a process of transformation from one based on security concerns to one in which economic issues and processes were dominant; this transformation has now been called into question by the return of security issues to dominate the headlines. Indeed, many observers have spoken of the *return* of the Cold War. International Relations, then, is in a state of turmoil with regards to what is the correct focus for study. This article seeks to trace the development of the discipline so as to outline the major approaches to studying international relations, and thereby to explain the major current debates within the discipline. This survey will identify two major historical schools of thought in the explanation of International Relations (idealism and realism), and will then examine the major areas of the subject in the light of this historical development.

THE NATURE OF INTERNATIONAL RELATIONS THEORY

Before this survey can be undertaken it is important to say a few words about the emergence of the subject of International Relations. The subject emerged as a separate discipline following the First World War, largely as a reaction to the carnage of that war, but more so because of a widespread feeling that the war had been an accident. Until that time, the study of International Relations had been undertaken within three other subject-areas: law, which dealt with the issues of how to outlaw war as well as the legal foundations for policies of neutrality and peaceful international intercourse; history, which concentrated upon detailed examinations of specific events and attempted to construct explanations of them; and philosophy, which was concerned with clarifying the role of the state in civil and world society. Yet, this diversification of effort was shattered by the events of World War One; this provides us with an opportunity to make a second introductory point, which concerns the relationship between the academic study and the object of that study. Put simply, it is incumbent on an academic discipline to explain the dominant issues within that subject-area. For example, the paradigm developed to explain the international system of the 1940s, 50s and 60s was replaced by one that claimed to explain more of the salient issues. This is the kind of issue raised by Thomas Kuhn in his work on paradigms,[1] and this article is based on the assumption that the study of international relations has been characterised by the existence of paradigms; further, it can be pointed out that the current situation is one in which competing paradigms vie for attention, each being able to explain parts of empirical reality but with no single paradigm being dominant. Before turning to examine the nature of the study of international relations it is necessary to turn to discuss this notion of paradigm by looking at how we relate evidence to theories; i.e. what is the relationship between our knowledge about the world and the reality we are trying to explain? This requires a discussion of terms such as theory, hypothesis and law; this discussion is essential since every kind of statement about International Relations reflects some kind of theoretical judgement on orientation. There is no more powerful theorist than he or she who states that they have no theory.

There is considerable imprecision concerning the term theory; to many it means a hypothesis, or even an argument, that can be in some way verified (or falsified) by the empirical material. I would like to argue that this is fundamentally flawed. The devices that we use to explain empirical material, can, following Waltz,[2] be divided into hypotheses and theories; each of these has a very different relationship to the empirical material. According to a very common view of this relationship, a theory is merely a collection of verified hypotheses, or laws, that apply to a particular behavioural phenomenon. This view is particularly powerful when it has what can be called a technological utility — that is that verified hypotheses offer us ways of achieving certain goals. The most obvious example of this is the knowledge derived from correlation coefficients. As Waltz writes: "It is then easy to believe that a real causal connection has been identified and measured, to think that the relation between an independent and a dependent variable has been established, and to forget that something has been said only about dots on a piece of paper and the regression line drawn through them."[3] Now, whilst high correlation coefficients may be very useful in practical terms they do not constitute an explanation; this is, then, a confusion of descriptive and explanatory knowledge.

This confusion is especially likely in subjects that permit a high degree of quantification and it is in this sense that the view of theory as a set of confirmed hypotheses is both popular and mistaken. This mistake rests on a basic confusion between what constitutes a description of empirical material and what constitutes an explanation of it. This problem, termed the 'inductivist illusion', is based on the premise that if we gather more and more data and can obtain strong correlations within this data, then we will arrive at knowledge. But, as Waltz has pointed out, the "belief that the pieces can be added up, that they can be treated as independent variables whose summed effects will account for a certain portion of a dependent variable's movement, rests on nothing more than faith."[4] This is because facts simply do not speak for themselves just as correlations neither prove causation nor contain their own explanation.

Theories, then, are not collections of verified hypotheses, or laws, they are devices that explain an empirical relationship. This position should not be confused with the positivist position so powerfully attacked by Keat and Urry,[5] since theories may consist of non-empirical observations. Under this view, theories differ fundamentally from hypotheses and laws in terms of their link with the empirical material. Whereas we can assess hypotheses and laws in terms of their validity, and thereby construct a direct link between them and empirical data, we evaluate theories in terms of the amount of behaviour that they can explain. Of course, theories may lead to the deduction of hypotheses, which may then be subjected to examination against the empirical data, but theories themselves cannot be proved to be true or false; they are either more or less powerful in their explanations, with the concept of explanatory power measured in terms of one theory's ability to explain more observed behaviour than its rivals. The criterion of empirical verification therefore applies to hypotheses and laws and not to theories. Hence one theory is replaced not by a 'truer' one, nor by one that contains more hypotheses, but by one that explains all that the original theory can and more. Theories are therefore replaced by ones with more explanatory power, ones that can better explain the relationship between verified hypotheses or laws. The relationship between theory and empirical material is, in this sense, an indirect one. It is important to remember that theories are related to empirical material in this indirect way, so that, whilst theories are neither true nor false, they do have the requirement of relating to verified hypotheses; in this way they can be distinguished from normative theories, that is theories that deal with questions of what should be the case. To summarise the argument thus far: the task of theory is to explain the relationship between verified hypotheses or laws with these hypotheses or laws being the part of the theory that relates directly to empirical material. Since facts do not speak for themselves, mere verified hypotheses cannot constitute explanations. Herein, of course, lies one of the major problems in the methodology of history since the existence of 'facts' can in no way lead the historian to induce an explanation; this is not to say that historians do not derive explanations, but they clearly must do so on the basis of deducing from (normally implicit) theories, or at least theoretical assumptions, the way both to arrange and choose the 'facts' and to link these to causal processes.

However, it is central to the argument of this article to establish that theories relate to the empirical material in a more direct way than has been outlined so far. This relates to the way in which theories themselves define the selection of empirical materials (and this is a significant development in the straight-forward positivist position). For Kuhn, a paradigm exists when a community of scholars adheres to a theory, or to a group of theories, to such an extent that this theory (or theories) dominates the subject-area. This paradigm performs a number of tasks that are critical to the relationship between theory and empirical material: the paradigm provides an exemplar for undertaking research; it defines the relevant data from the available facts; it provides criteria for distinguishing between relevant and irrelevant questions; it provides a route for the subject-area to follow, so that there is no need to return to first principles. To use Kuhn's terms, it sets the relevant 'puzzles' and allows the scientist to become a 'puzzle-solver'; the subject-area is a 'normal science'.

A paradigm, then, provides exactly the kind of criteria that allows the scholars in a field to distinguish between relevant and irrelevant facts. In this sense it has a direct relationship to the empirical material, in that it defines the relevant facts, and thereby the central issues to be explained by theory. As Kuhn writes: "Paradigms gain their status because they are more successful than their competitors in solving a few problems that the group of practitioners has come to recognise as acute."[6] This is the way in which theory, in a normal science, relates most directly to the empirical material. Indeed, paradigms are not replaced by more accurate ones, they are superseded by paradigms that explain more of the observable behaviour. Since, of course, paradigms themselves determine the relevance of empirical material, competing paradigms may exist, with each paradigm focusing on different behaviour, and different questions. Kuhn argues that normal science is not characterised by disputes between competing paradigms, rather it sees one paradigm dominating the subject-area. It must be stressed that Kuhn is not a relativist, although this is something that he has often been accused of. Kuhn does not argue that it is impossible to choose between competing theories, precisely because there exists the link between theory, hypotheses, and empirical material. Thus, although competing paradigms do not focus on exactly the same material and do not see exactly the same questions as central to the task of explanation, there is a corpus of behaviour that no explanation can ignore. Paradigms, therefore, do not prevent the resolution of differences between them, they merely obstruct this process. In principle, then, the resolution of disputes between competing paradigms is possible, thus avoiding the problem of relativism.

Paradigms therefore structure a subject-area by defining the relevant questions and offering methods of delineating the data from the mass of empirical material. The theory, or group of theories, at the heart of a paradigm will both determine the questions to be explained and yet will have to be able to explain the central issues of the discipline. It is exactly by this dialectical process that a subject-area develops.

THE DEVELOPMENT OF THE SUBJECT

It is instructive to examine the subject-area of International Relations in this light. Indeed, as Richard Little has noted: "The emergence of International Relations as an independent discipline came not as a challenge to the sovereignty of philosophy and an attempt to resolve on-going philosophical debate, but as a response to real world events."[7] The real world event that, above all others, led to the emergence of the discipline was the First World War. Before this, the study of International Relations had been undertaken within the aegis of either history or philosophy, although, of course, law also provided a rather specialised perspective. Since the emergence of the separate discipline in the period immediately following the First World War, it is normally argued that two major phases have existed; these may be loosely labelled paradigms. In chronological order, these phases were: idealism, which dominated the discipline in the interwar years, and realism, which received its initial statement in E. H. Carr's *The Twenty Years' Crisis*[8] and which characterised the discipline from the period of the Second World War to the 1960s. Since the 1960s, realism has come under attack from an approach called behaviouralism. The current situation is one in which the realist paradigm, or versions of it, has strong adherents in the discipline, being opposed by what can be called the transnationalist paradigm. In the mid-1980s it is simply not the case that either one of these approaches dominates the discipline, as will be discussed below.

Idealism was, naturally, largely preoccupied with avoiding a repetition of wars such as the First World War. As Bull has argued, the distinctive characteristic of idealism was the belief in progress: "the belief, in particular, that the system of international relations that had given rise to the First World War was capable of being transformed into a fundamentally more peaceful and just world order; that under the impact of the awakening of democracy, the growth of 'the international mind', the development of the League of Nations, the good works of men of peace or the enlightenment spread by their own teachings, it was in fact being transformed; and that their responsibility . . . was to assist this march of progress to overcome the ignorance, the prejudices, the ill-will, and the sinister interests that stood in its way."[9] Given this orientation, the discipline concentrated on developing and publicising techniques for the peaceful resolution of crises. Hence, most attention was paid to international law and to international organisations. Rational decision-makers wished to avoid war so the task of International Relations was to provide the mechanisms necessary to ensure this. The First World War was seen as occurring because of misperception and accident; the League of Nations was therefore based on assumptions as to the role of mediation and the peace-enhancing characteristics of democracy. Combined with these beliefs was the powerful manifesto of Wilson's Fourteen Points. Taken together these viewpoints formed the basis of idealism.

The growing disparity between these views and real-world events in the 1930s, primarily, of course, the advent of the Second World War, led to a re-examination of the discipline. This re-examination is most cogently expressed in Carr's *The Twenty Years' Crisis*[10] and Morgenthau's *Politics Among Nations*.[11] Carr's book contains a most powerful attack on idealism, an attack based on the idea that the science of International Relations was in its early stages. In this period, Carr argues, any discipline is likely to be characterised by utopianism, that is by a concentration on what ought to be rather than on what is. He argues that

the overwhelming purpose which dominated and inspired the pioneers of the new science was to obviate a recurrence of this disease [war] of the international body politic. The passionate desire to prevent war determined the whole initial course and direction of the study. Like other infant sciences, the science of international politics has been markedly and frankly utopian. It has been in the initial stage in which wishing prevails over thinking, generalisation over observation, and in which little attempt is made at a critical analysis of existing facts.[12]

It was exactly this growing disparity between events and idealism that provided an opportunity, for the first time, for the critical analysis of international relations.

This critical analysis was labelled by Carr 'realism', and its most powerful statement occurs in Morgenthau's seminal book, *Politics Among Nations.* For Morgenthau, International Relations had to start from a realisation that the international political behaviour of states had its origins in immutable laws of nature. On this basis, he offers a theory of international politics, the purpose of which is "to bring order and meaning to a mass of phenomena which without it would remain disconnected and unintelligible."[13] This theory not only has to be consistent within itself, it also has to be consistent with the facts. Here again we see the relationship between theory and empirical material; the material gives rise to the revision of theory, the theory determines the facts to be explained, yet the theory must be consistent with the major empirical developments.

Morgenthau's theory is based on six principles. The first of these, and the most fundamental, is that political behaviour is governed "by objective laws that have their roots in human nature."[14] These laws cannot be altered by human beings and can therefore be challenged only at the risk of failure. Secondly, realism offers an explanation of international relations by concentrating on power. As Morgenthau writes: "We assume that statesmen think and act in terms of interest defined as power."[15] Thirdly, realism does not endow the concept of power with one fixed meaning; power can relate to any process by which individuals seek to dominate other individuals. Fourthly, whilst the realist is aware of the role of morality in international political behaviour, it is important to note that universal moral principles cannot be applied to international relations; there can be no political morality without prudence, especially when seemingly moral action could lead to the destruction of the state. Fifthly, realism does not identify the moral aspirations of any one state with universal morality; hence, it can offer a means of judging all states' behaviour. Finally, the realist sees the political sphere as autonomous, in that other modes of thought cannot explain the central areas of behaviour.

Morgenthau's statement of realism had an extensive impact on both the discipline and the practice of international relations. For the academic it offered a way of relating, deductively, theory and practice. For the politician, as Rothstein points out, it was popular because it "encapsulated what they took for granted, especially after the failures of the 1930s and during the height of the cold war."[16] Indeed, he argues that realism was "the doctrine which provided the intellectual frame of reference for the foreign policy establishment for something like twenty years ... it did determine the categories by which they assessed the external world and the state of mind with which they approached prevailing problems."[17]

However, by the late 1950s realism itself was under attack from what can be called behaviouralism, that is a school of thought based on developing knowledge about observable behaviour. For this school of thought, realism had a fundamental epistemological flaw since it started from (unobservable) fixed laws of human behaviour and 'explained' observable events from this standpoint. Although behaviouralism took many different forms, the clearest examples of it are provided by the decision-making approach started by Richard Synder[18] and the systems-theory approach introduced by Morton Kaplan.[19] For Snyder, foreign policy behaviour was not to be explained by any rational assessments of interest defined as power (as were required by Morgenthau), but by the *subjective choices,* based on the definition of the situation, of the decision-makers. For Snyder, explanation did not consist of seeing these choices as examples of fixed laws of nature, but by undertaking empirical investigation to see how decision-makers defined situations.

Similarly, for Kaplan, understanding the behaviour of great powers was not to be arrived at through seeing it as the characteristic behaviour of states located in an immutable web of objective laws, but as determined by more specific, and thereby changing, characteristics of the structure of the system. Hence Kaplan constructs a series of theoretical models of the system and in later work outlined alternative theoretical models. The contrast between his work and that of Morgenthau is subtle but significant.

Behaviouralism's attack on realism was by no means universally accepted, and the realists, or, as they became known, the traditionalists, mounted a very strong counter-attack. This lead to a famous debate, although it was hardly a debate, between Bull and Kaplan.[20] This so-called 'Great Debate' was only one form of attack on behaviouralism however: potentially a much more serious one was the post-behaviouralist attack. This attack had two main aspects: first, a criticism of behaviouralism's absence of moral and normative content. By concentrating on what is, and by confining theory to an explanation of this, behaviouralism is seen as being devoid of moral content. Given the role of academics in the United States in the planning, and explanation, of the Vietnam War, this is an understandable criticism of behaviouralism. The second aspect of the post-behavioural critique is a rejection of the inductive approach to developing knowledge. This position is most clearly expressed in Oran Young's celebrated attack on inductivism.[21] It has also been a central argument in the critiques of what is probably the best example of inductive research – Singer's Correlates of War Project.[22] In other words, this criticism argues that merely accumulating empirical evidence cannot provide the basis of explanation, a point already outlined.

STATE-CENTRIC VERSUS TRANSNATIONALIST APPROACHES

In the literature of International Relations it is common to see these differing schools of thought (idealism, realism, behaviouralism and post-behaviouralism) as competing paradigms; this, though, is an over-simplification, since only the first two achieved anything like the degree of theoretical dominance in the discipline required by Kuhn's notion of a paradigm. Indeed, behaviouralism and post-behaviouralism by themselves do not necessarily focus on different aspects of International Relations then do idealism and realism; there is nothing intrinsic to behaviouralism that forces it to study anything different to that studied by realists – one can easily envisage realist behaviouralists. Thus, for example, Kaplan and Snyder have more in common with Morgenthau or Carr than is commonly accepted. In this sense, the so-called 'Great Debate' was largely a debate about questions of how you study international relations – with the issue of what the discipline was being accepted and agreed on by the protagonists. The current identity crisis, then, is not simply one based on the issue of which methodology is appropriate; it relates to the fundamental issues of what is to be studied. This can be most clearly indicated by looking at the question of the state in International Relations.

In their slightly different ways, and certainly by different means, idealism, realism, behaviouralism and post-behaviouralism accepted what can be called the state-centric viewpoint. To this extent, the debates between the various orientations were confined to the question of how best to study the behaviour of states. Each can be seen as part of this wider paradigm of the state-centric approach, which dominated the study of International Relations until the mid-1970s when a competing view – transnationalism – emerged. The current problems of the discipline emerge not from issues of methodology but from the inability of either state-centrism or transnationalism to explain the central empirical questions of International Relations.

The dominance of the assumptions of the state-centric paradigm has been very clearly illustrated in an unpublished paper by Handelman, Vasquez, O'Leary and Coplin.[23] Their paper tests a very simple hypothesis, which is that "quantitative and other systematic studies of International Relations have been dominated by a (sic) over-riding state-centred power-politics paradigm, a paradigm which accepts a view of the world most notably advanced by Hans J. Morgenthau."[24] Through quantitative analysis they show that the assumptions of the state-centric approach were shared by approaches that seemed to challenge it: "Reviewing the literature of the 1960s, we find a number of schools which appear to challenge the Morgenthau paradigm because they use different concepts. However ... all ... must be considered elaborations of the initial paradigm ... In effect the International Relations literature on (sic) the 1960s was a series of variations on the Morgenthau paradigm."[25]

In a later article,[26] Vasquez argues that quantitative International Relations research, although seen as an alternative (behaviouralism) to realism, in fact is based on the three basic assumptions of realism (and, one may add, idealism): (i) Nation-states are the most important actors in international relations; (ii) there is a sharp distinction between domestic politics and international politics; and, (iii) the focus of International Relations is the study of power and peace. Whereas behaviouralist analysis would be expected to analyse behaviour *per se,* Vasquez found that even behaviouralism examined international relations in terms of realist assumptions. Thus, despite the superficial differences between the 'rival' approaches of behaviouralism and realism, they shared a much more powerful set of assumptions.

To summarise the argument thus far: International Relations, from its inception as a separate discipline to the early 1970s, was based on a state-centric power-politics framework. Thus, whilst idealists might disagree over how to get peace, each saw states as actors, and war as the central problem. Whilst behaviouralism might criticise the methodology of realism, it still saw the central behaviour to be explained as the power-political behaviour of states. Again, whilst post-behaviouralism might criticise either the inductiveness of much behaviouralism or the lack of any normative content, it too was concerned with the security policies of states.

In this regard, the major change in the study of International Relations was not the movement from idealism to realism, nor from realism to behaviouralism (the most frequently cited turning points), but developed as a response to a set of events that occurred in the early and middle 1970s. In this sense, the early and middle 1970s was a period of significant importance in International Relations; again, we see the way in which empirical events lead to a change in the way the subject is studied. What is special about this period, though, is that it seemed to challenge the very assumptions that lay at the heart of realist and behaviouralist analysis.

The events of the 1970s can usefully be separated into three categories: those concerned with the structure of the global system; those concerned with the units of international society; and those concerned with the processes of International Relations. Rather than discuss each in detail, a brief summary of the major events in each category will be offered.

At the global level, the major event was the seeming break-up of bipolarity (US-Soviet dominance) as a structural characteristic. On the one hand, this was due to the fragmentation of the two-bloc system; on the other, it resulted from the rise of other actors. Thus, many academics saw the beginnings of a trend that could lead lo a multipolar (or a tripolar) world, with China, a united Western Europe, and Japan all challenging the domination of the United States and the Soviet Union. This process was seen to be all the more powerful because of the likely spread of nuclear weapons to other states; hence, the literature was full of speculation about what life would be like in a world of, say, twenty nuclear powers. Added to this was the clear increase in the economic capabilities of great, as distinct from super, powers. Finally, the superpowers themselves seemed to be engaged in a transformation of their relationship into one of detente, as marked by the Non-Proliferation Treaty, by the Berlin agreement, by the Conference on Security and Co-operation in Europe, and, above all, by the Strategic Arms Limitation Talks. In this environment the suitability of the assumptions of realism and of much power-based behaviouralism were called into question. Probably the best examples of this are Alastair Buchan's *The End of the Postwar Era*,[27] and Seyom Brown's *New Forces in World Politics*,[28] both published in 1974. Each of these books talks about the end of Cold War alignments in the system, with Buchan concentrating on the new world balance of power, and Brown focusing on the disintegration of the Cold War coalitions.

At the level of the changing processes of International Relations there was one fundamental transformation which, it was argued, was taking place. This was the replacement of security interests by economic interests as the dominant issues in International Relations; obviously this was related to both the rise of other economic powers and to the decline of US-Soviet rivalry, but it was also more fundamental. For many writers, the early 1970s saw the transformation of the East-West cleavage into a North-South cleavage. The traditional 'high politics' issues were no longer the dominant ones, rather the system was split on economic, or 'low politics' issues. The clearest example was, of course, the oil crisis of 1973-74, which was seen as ushering in a new phase of International Relations.

Both of these areas of change affected the units of international society. What had been seen as essentially a state-based system was being transformed by two processes: on the one hand, the distinction between domestic and international politics was fast breaking down; on the other, new actors, non-state actors, seemed increasingly to be dominating certain, primarily economic, issue-areas. The first of these processes resulted in states no longer being able to control key areas of domestic policy; thus, the traditional areas of economic policy were evidently affected, and in many cases determined, by external factors. In this sense the legal concept of sovereignty was no longer as relevant as autonomy. What had previously been seen as a relatively sharp divide between domestic and international politics was now seen as much less clear-cut. The second process compounded the first in that many of the external actors that could affect what had previously been seen as domestic issues were not states. Hence, in key areas, states did not dominate; the most obvious example was in oil where OPEC and the seven large multinationals exerted a significant influence on the domestic policies of industrialised and developing states.

The effect of these changes was to call seriously into question the central assumptions of the discipline of International Relations. If states were no longer the dominant actors in certain issue-areas, if power, specifically military power, was not the focus of study, and if the units of international society were no longer autonomous in areas of central importance, then, it was argued, could the state-centric view of International Relations explain the major events in the real world? The response to this situation was the development of an alternative paradigm, one usually labelled transnationalism.

This new paradigm has essentially two major components each of which takes account of part of the changes in International Relations, but which together constitute a powerful alternative to the state-centric view. The first of these relates to the growing interdependence between national societies and is best expressed in Morse's book, *Modernization and the Transformation of International Relations,*[29] published in 1976. Morse argues that systemic economic interdependence has resulted in a situation where: "Traditional assumptions concerning alliances, the use of force, the role of economic diplomacy, the processes of foreign policy decision making... are... part of a paradigm of international affairs that is no longer adequate for explaining contemporary conditions."[30] For Morse, interdependence represents a transformation of international relations whereby foreign policies "... have become increasingly centred on low policies associated with the achievement of economic growth, but frequently inter-meshed with a new form of transcendentalism that reflects the incapacity of governments to perform effectively."[31] The end result is that international politics is no longer distinct in terms of its contents; it increasingly merges with domestic politics.

The second, and major, strand of the transnational approach is that which focuses on the types of actor involved in International Relations. The main argument here is that states are no longer the dominant actors in certain issue-areas. The first detailed statement of this position was Keohane and Nye's *Transnational Relations and World Politics,*[32] in which they examined the role of a variety of non-state actors and concluded that the state-centric paradigm simply could not deal with contemporary international relations. Following this study, transnational relations developed into a minor industry, with the two most significant contributions being Mansbach, Ferguson and Lampert's *The Web of World Politics,*[33] and Mansbach and Vasquez's, *In Search of Theory.*[34] The former undertook quantitative analysis to determine the percentage of non-state activity in international relations, and found that non-state actors appeared in 56 per cent of international behaviour.[35] The latter was concerned to develop an alternative to the state-centric paradigm.

Certainly, these attempts to transform the discipline were strongly resisted — most trenchantly in Northedge's article, 'Transnationalism: the American Illusion'[36] — but it is clear that by the late 1970s this alternative paradigm was largely accepted, especially in the United States. Even where it was not accepted, significant modifications were made to the state-centric paradigm, so as to reflect the requirements of explaining a changed international system. In this sense it can be argued that the discipline was fundamentally transformed in the 1970s by the need to explain new phenomena. By the end of the decade the assumptions of the discipline had changed; the state-centric paradigm was clearly inadequate and was, therefore, either augmented by further assumptions or replaced by the transnationalist paradigm.

THE CURRENT STATE OF THE DISCIPLINE

In this light, events since 1979 appear to be particularly problematic. This is for the very simple reason that neither the state-centric nor the transnationalist paradigm seems capable of explaining the central events of international relations. Whereas the East-West split, based on the security interests of states, clearly dominated post-war international relations for twenty-five years, and whereas it was commonly accepted that this had been replaced by a North-South cleavage, based on economic issues, in the mid-1970s, neither view can account for the current position. It is in this sense that the question of the return of the Cold War is perplexing. Of course, each of the paradigms could offer an explanation, but neither is convincing, although there has been much in the way of a revival of realist thinking, which has been termed 'neo-realism'. It is difficult to accept either the argument that this is merely a temporary return to the dominance of security issues, or the view that the period of the 1970s was itself the aberration. Rather, it seems that the international political system has been transformed in that economic factors are of central importance (although Marxist scholars would argue that this has always been the case). Yet, at the same time, security issues have simply not been removed from centre-stage. Just as interdependence is so obviously a 'fact' of contemporary international relations, just as non-state actors are of critical importance in a wide range of international activity, so the cleavage caused by US-Soviet rivalry is a central structural feature of the international system. In the late 1970s it made sense to assume that the rise of non-state actors and the predominance of economic issues represented a once-and-for-all change, one requiring new theory to explain it. Thus the new paradigm competed with the old and, for many, was clearly preferable in that it could accommodate the dominant forms of behaviour. Yet the return of features that bear more resemblance to the world of the 1950s than to the world of the 1970s calls this into question. At the same time, the state-centric approach has demonstrably failed to be able to explain the world of the 1970s. The subject of International Relations is, therefore, one in which much debate is going on as to what should be the main areas of study. Whilst this may seem on the surface to be a sign of weakness or self-doubt, it is, in fact, a very healthy intellectual sign, in that it makes the subject very concerned with questions of relevance. Not surprisingly, the subject is taught in a variety of ways, with the following areas often being the titles of courses in international relations at Universities and Polytechnics:

(a) International History

The study of recent (c20th) events, concentrating on the major structural features of international society such as the causes of the First and Second World Wars, the Cold War, Detente, De-Colonization, the rise of economic factors, etc.

(b) Strategic Studies

The study of the causes of war, and the ways wars are undertaken. This area usually includes an examination of nuclear weapons, the history of US-Soviet arms control, nuclear proliferation, and European defence issues.

(c) Theories of International Relations

Such a course is often included along with a basic survey of international history in an introductory course on International Relations. It is also common to find a specialist course looking at the major theories of international politics.

(d) Foreign Policy Analysis

This area is concerned with outlining general theoretical approaches to the analysis of the foreign policy of states. These approaches are often seen to apply to most, if not all, types of states, and look at how decisions are made and implemented. Such a course will usually examine in detail the foreign policies of a number of states.

(e) International Political Economy

This area has been an extremely important one since the oil crisis of 1973 brought economic issues to the fore (although many would argue that it had always been important, and had merely been neglected!). It studies the major processes and structures in the international economy.

(f) International Law

As the title suggests, such a course looks at the ways in which international law is made, how it is applied and how it is adjudicated.

(g) Integration Theory

This was one of the main growth areas in the discipline in the 1950s and 1960s, as it examined the ways in which states form international economic and technical organisations. It is now often concerned with the major example of this process, the European Community.

(h) International Institutions/International Organisation

Courses with these titles are concerned with the workings of international bodies such as the United Nations and the League of Nations, especially insofar as the existence of the organisation effects the behaviour of its constituent member-states.

(i) Conflict Studies/Peace Studies

Arising out of the widely felt dissatisfaction with the neglect of many moral issues in conventional strategic studies courses, there have been a number of courses started which explicitly focus on how to obtain peace, rather than on how wars occur.

There are, of course, many other aspects to the study of International Relations, especially given the fact that the subject is constantly concerned with the need to relate to and explain contemporary events. As was pointed out above, there are major methodological divides in the way the subject is taught and researched in this country. These largely reflect the debates in social science generally, and tend to concern the possibility of utilising scientific methods in the study of International Relations. In the United States, social scientific analysis is far more popular in International Relations teaching and research than it is in Britain, where the focus has reflected the subject's origins in philosophy, law and, above all, history.

One issue that is raised by the very structural givens of international society, and which provides one of the greatest intellectual challenges of the subject, is that of the linkage between the behaviour of the members (normally assumed to be states) of international society and the structure of international society. Because international society has, unlike domestic societies, no government above the constituent states, it is said to be anarchical. This poses the question of whether the foreign policies of states reflect the conscious choices of those who make the decisions or whether the nature of international anarchy (no government, and no independently enforceable international law) dictates how states react. For example, the lack of a world government puts states in the same position to one another as individuals would be without government in society. This means that they have to ensure their own defence from attack and in trying to achieve this they may increase the feelings of insecurity of others. Similarly, states seem to behave differently according to how many great powers there are in international society (is the system multipolar — five or more great powers — or bipolar?) In each type of international system, the characteristic ways of resolving conflicts and balancing the power of other states is different. Now, why this is especially relevant is that this line of argument leads to the question of whether the existence of nuclear weapons has kept the peace since 1945 or whether the peace has been kept because the system has become bipolar. This leads to the issue of what will be the effect of the likely spread of nuclear weapons to other states in the late 1980s and early 1990s. This is an example of the kind of issue that is driving current research and thinking about international relations.

International Relations, then, has had a very interesting past. What this brief survey has shown is that the subject has always been very explicitly concerned with explaining (rather than merely describing) the major features of international society. As these features have changed so has International Relations had to develop new theories to explain them. Since the 1960s, realism has been under attack, more in the United States than in Britain, with the major challenge coming in the 1970s with the rise of economic factors to a position of dominance in international relations. Yet, the rise of the Second Cold War in the early 1980s has led to a resurgence of realism. The study of international relations in the second half of the 1980s looks like being exceptionally stimulating as the subject grapples with the task of explaining a dynamic, turbulent and dangerous world.

124

1. See especially T. Kuhn: The Structure of Scientific Revolutions. Second Edition. (Chicago: University of Chicago Press, 1970).

2. See K. Waltz: Theory of International Politics (Reading, Mass.: Addison-Wesley, 1979).

3. Ibid., 2.

4. Ibid., 4.

5. See R. Keat and J. Urry: Social Theory as Science (London: Routledge and Kegan Paul, 1975), especially chapter one.

6. T. Kuhn, op. cit., 23.

7. R. Little, 'The Evolution of International Relations as a Social Science', in R. Kent and G. Neilsson (eds.): The Study and Teaching of International Relations (London: Frances Pinter, 1980), 5.

8. E. H. Carr: The Twenty Years' Crisis (London: Macmillan, 1939). (Quotations from the second edition, 1945).

9. H. Bull: 'The Theory of International Politics 1919-1969', in B. Porter (ed.), The Aberystwyth Papers (London: Oxford University Press, 1972), 35.

10. Carr, op. cit.

11. H. Morgenthau: Politics Among Nations (New York: Knopf, 1948) (all quotations are from the fifth edition, published in 1973).

12. Carr, op. cit., 8.

13. Morgenthau, op. cit., 3.

14. Ibid., 4.

15. Ibid., 5.

16. R. Rothstein: 'On the Costs of Realism', Political Science Quarterly Vol. LXXXVII, (1972), 348.

17. Ibid.

18. See R. Snyder, H. Bruck and B. Sapin: Foreign Policy Decision Making (New York: Free Press, 1962).

19. See M. Kaplan: System and Process in International Politics (New York: Wiley, 1957).

20. For Bull's original article, Kaplan's response, and a variety of other contributions, see K. Knorr and J. Rosenau (eds.): Contending Approaches to International Politics (Princeton, N.J.: Princeton University Press, 1969).

21. See O. Young: 'Professor Russett: Industrious Tailor to a Naked Emperor', World Politics, Vol. 21 (1969), 486-511.

22. See, for example, the chapters by Job and Ostrom, Duvall and Starr, along with the rejoinder by Singer, in F. Hoole and D. Zinnes (eds.): Quantitative International Politics (New York: Praeger, 1976).

23. J. Handelman, J. Vasquez, M. O'Leary and W. Coplin: 'Color it Morgenthau: a Data-Based Assessment of Quantitative International Relations Research', Prince Research Studies, Syracuse University, 1973.

24. Ibid., 1.

25. Ibid., 31.

26. J. Vasquez: 'Colouring it Morgenthau: New Evidence for an Old Thesis on Quantitative International Politics', British Journal of International Studies, Vol. 4 (1979), 210-228.

27. A. Buchan: The End of the Postwar Era (London: Weidenfeld and Nicolson, 1974).

28. S. Brown: New Forces in World Politics (Washington, D.C.: Brookings, 1974).

29. E. Morse: Modernization and the Transformation of International Relations (New York: Free Press, 1976).

30. Ibid., XVI.

31. Ibid., 107.

32. R. Keohane and J. Nye: Transnational Relations and World Politics (Cambridge, Mass.: Harvard University Press, 1972).

33. R. Mansbach, Y. Ferguson and D. Lampert: The Web of World Politics (Englewood Cliffs, Mass.: Prentice-Hall, 1976).

34. R. Mansbach and J. Vasquez: In Search of Theory (New York: Columbia University Press, 1981).

35. Mansbach, Ferguson and Lampert op. cit., 276.

36. F. Northedge: 'Transnationalism: The American Illusion', Millennium, Vol. 5 (1), (1976), 21-27.

SELECT BIBLIOGRAPHY

G. Allison: Essence of Decision (Boston, Mass.: Little, Brown, 1971).

S. Brown: New Forces in World Politics (Washington, D.C.: Brookings, 1974).

P. Calvocoressi: World Politics Since 1945, Fourth Edition (London: Longmans, 1982).

J. Dougherty and R. Pfaltzgraff: Contending Theories of International Relations, Second Edition (New York: Harper and Row, 1980).

J. Frankel: International Relations in a Changing World (Oxford: Oxford University Press, 1979).

K. Holsti: International Politics, Fourth Edition (Englewood Cliffs, N.J.: Prentice-Hall, 1983).

L. Jensen: Explaining Foreign Policy (Englewood Cliffs, N.J.: Prentice-Hall, 1982).

R. Keohane and J. Nye (eds.): Transnational Relations and World Politics (Cambridge, Mass.: Harvard University Press, 1972).

R. Keohane and J. Nye: Power and Interdependence (Boston, Mass.: Little, Brown, 1977).

R. Mansbach and J. Vasquez: In Search of Theory (New York: Columbia University Press, 1981).

H. Morgenthau: Politics Among Nations, Fifth Edition (New York: Knopf, 1978).

P. Reynolds: An Introduction to International Relations, Second Edition (London: Longmans, 1980).

M. Smith, R. Little and M. Shackleton (eds.): Perspectives on World Politics (London: Croom Helm, 1981).

T. Taylor (ed.): Approaches and Theory in International Relations (London: Longmans, 1978).

K. Waltz: Man, The State and War (New York: Columbia University Press, 1959).

K. Waltz: Theory of International Politics (Reading, Mass.: Addison-Wesley, 1979).

Political Geography

Graham E. Smith

Political Geography is simultaneously one of the oldest yet youngest branches of geographical enquiry. With its somewhat chequered and unique history, the subject has moved from a period just before and immediately after the First World War when it had much to say about political problems and issues, to a sterile era in the 1950s and 1960s when research was accomplished by and for political geographers who took little cognisance of thinking in either mainstream Human Geography or Political Science. In return for its inward looking stance, it attracted little or no interest from beyond its narrowly conceived and rigidly defended disciplinary boundaries. Since then, however, Political Geography has undergone a revival: textbooks on the subject, many novel in approach and subject matter, pour off the printing presses on both sides of the Atlantic. Whether or not the subject's recent renaissance has meant that it has undergone 'a quiet and moderate revolution' as some would contend or that it is still in need of 'a major overhaul' is clearly central to assessing the current state of Political Geography. Few geographers would however contest the view that although Political Geography still needs to reassess its content, coherence and direction, it has much to offer a human geography which tackles those substantive political issues which are focal to any thriving social science. Equally, the more recent interest shown by political scientists in 'territorial politics', particularly in relation to urban government, state-building and political regionalism, is further evidence that the subject has much to offer the study of politics.

EARLY DEVELOPMENTS

While the ancient, medieval and post-Renaissance philosophers were often interested in the geographical bases of the state, the origins of Political Geography as an organised field of academic enquiry can be traced to the organisation of Geography itself as a branch of scholarship in late nineteenth century Germany. Friedrich Ratzel (1844-1904) was the founding father of the subject and the offspring discipline was very much a child of its times, influenced by the fashionable concepts of environmental determinism (the notion that human developments are responses to the characteristics, controls and stimuli of the physical environment) and Darwinism. The state was given a central position on the geographical stage and conceived as an organic entity, endowed with a variety of environmental and cultural assets and struggling for growth or survival in a competitive international environment.[1]

In Britain, where the growth of Geography was slower and less certain, political considerations, (other than those of exploration for imperial purposes), were less prominent. Indeed the late nineteenth century foundation of a School of Geography at Oxford under Mackinder produced objections that his interest in politics might degrade or subvert the nascent discipline. Nevertheless, in 1904 Mackinder[2] produced what must be the most widely read of all geographical expositions; the 'Heartland' thesis[3] which evolved from his identifications of a supposed Russian 'Geographical Pivot of History'. It attempted to interpret world politics, past and future, in terms of an expansionist and unassailable global power centre. It represented an attempt to place the fruits of its author's geographical insights at the disposal of Western policy-makers and though its bases and predictions were dubious and sketchy, it may well have influenced Nazi policy and post-1945 American outlooks more than British policy. It certainly sparked public geopolitical debate and in some ways anticipated the often sinister use of geographical arguments as tools of state policy.

As well as stimulating Mackinder to redefine his 'Heartland' concept, the collapse of the European imperial dynasties in the aftermath of the 1914-18 war produced more practical and purposeful opportunities for political geographers to demonstrate the value of their expertise. Most notably, the chief American territorial specialist at the Versailles peace negotiations, Isaiah Bowman, applied his talents to the thorny problem of reconstructing the political map of Europe according to the fashionable principle of national self-determination. In his *The New World* of 1921 he provided an optimistic description of the post-war world and its problems.[4] The Versailles negotiations also sparked considerable academic debate, well-intentioned if naïve, upon the nature of international boundaries and the factors which should influence the construction of 'ideal' boundaries – raising questions of whether boundaries should aim to separate national communities or be drawn so as to necessitate contacts.

Working at the intra-national level, C. B. Fawcett anticipated much modern thinking relating to regionalism in his *Provinces of England* of 1919.[5] Influenced perhaps by the earlier Fabian socialist discussions on administrative reform and by the Irish Home Rule issue, he argued against state centralisation and in favour of a strong devolution of power to the English provinces, devoting great effort to the delimitation of provincial boundaries.

Thus, in the first third of this century, political geographers of various outlooks formed part of a youthful, vigorous and influential, if diffuse, academic community, even though the core, aims and methodologies of Political Geography remained rather obscure. The second third of the century witnessed a failure to capitalise on the lively beginnings, the stigmatisation and virtual collapse of the discipline and then, the establishment of sounder foundations for future developments.

In the Germany of the interwar years the political climate resulted in the strand of Political Geography which was concerned with the grander strategies of state policy being reforged into a grotesque weapon of propaganda, if not of policy. It is perhaps ironic that while a number of modern politicians — Henry Kissinger not the least — freely invoke the language and concepts of geopolitics, the topic of geopolitics is a virtual outcast within the subject which gave it birth. The reasons are easily identified. The more wayward and improbable of Ratzel's ideas relating to the state were developed firstly by Kjellen, a Swedish geographer, and then by Gen. Haushofer, a leading German traveller, academic and disciple of Hess. Nazi propagandists found in this subjectively revamped *Geopolitik* of Haushofer and his disciples, a tool which could be used to provide (spurious) intellectual justification for national paranoia, territorial claims and geopolitical objectives. The actual influence of geopolitical conclusions on Nazi war policy is uncertain but misleading geopolitical rhetoric and accompanying trick maps were prominent in the Nazi media.[6]

While the distinction between Political Geography as a field of academic description and analysis and *Geopolitik* with its perversion of facts for political ends was quite clearcut, the outraged reactions of Western scholars did not always discriminate between the two fields. As one American commentator remarked ' . . . anything that could be branded geopolitics became much "too hot to handle".'[7]

While geopolitics was paving the way for its near extinction, Political

Geography was preoccupied with empirical studies, particularly those concerned with international boundaries as facets of the cultural and economic landscape. The theoretical bases of the discipline remained hazy and despite the early stimulus which Fawcett had provided, the intra-national level of enquiry was neglected and workers were almost exclusively concerned with the state, its capital, margins and ethnic problems. Equally enervating was the failure to explore the concepts of Political Science or to forge partnerships and exchanges of ideas with related subjects. Though working on the doorstep of Political Science, political geographers seemed oblivious to what might be happening within the threshold. In fairness to the geographers, at this stage Political Science did not necessarily have a great deal to offer, other than indications of interest. The productive exchanges of ideas only resulted when both Geography and Political Science had undergone their individual but comparable conceptual and methodological revolutions.

THE 1950s AND 1960s: THE WILDERNESS YEARS

As the most unfashionable branch of Geography in the immediate postwar period, Political Geography was faced with the mammoth task of overcoming its unsavoury links with *Geopolitik*. By remaining firmly within the geographical fold and thus not delving into Politics, political geographers attempted to pursue a less controversial course for their studies. Unfortunately, while other branches of Geography were beginning to draw upon the ideas and methods already in existence in their related sister social and natural sciences, Political Geography was turning its back on what progress had been made in the field of Political Science. As a consequence, it remained apolitical and heavily laden with description because of this omission of political considerations.

During the fifties and sixties, theoretical and conceptual developments were few and far between. Indeed, the only major innovation produced to advance thinking in Political Geography were the works of the early functionalist school. Dominated by Hartshorne, Gottmann and Jones, these functionalist approaches to spatio-political phenomena continued to focus more or less exclusively on the state. Hartshorne's much quoted 10,000 word paper was concerned with the *raison d'être* of the state.[8] Focusing on the state's viability, he identified two conflicting and dynamic forces in its spatial composition — the centripetal, which binds the state together, and the centrifugal, which reflects disunity. Geographical factors such as location, distance, barriers to spatial interaction and regional diversity received systematic treatment, while only passing reference was given to the role of decision-makers and differences in social structure in enhancing or prohibiting the state's integration. According to Hartshorne, for the political geographer, 'the degree of vertical unification within any horizontal segment concerns us only as a factor aiding or handicapping regional unification.'[9] Although such a contribution gave political geographers a relatively cohesive focus from which other facets of state viability could be scrutinised, latterly it has been recognised as a rather over-simplified and generalised view of a state's existence mainly because of its failure to consider the whole range of sub-state conflicts.

Although the earlier contributions of Gottmann and Jones were not exclusively concerned with applying their functional approaches to the state, it is nevertheless evident that they were preoccupied with it. According to Gottmann, the division of the world into organised spaces is a function of degrees of accessibility, determined by two opposing forces, circulation and iconography, respectively similar to Hartshorne's notion of centrifugal and centripetal.[10] The former was essentially related to interactions within space which included the movement of ideas, commodities and people while the latter referred to locational symbols. In attempting to build upon this paradigm and that of Hartshorne's viability of the state-area, Jones' *A Unified Field Theory* represented an attempt to link 'political idea' with 'state-area'.[11] A theoretical chain linking political idea-decision-movement-field-political area was designed, primarily to identify how political processes defined spatial organisations. Such a holistic approach placed behaviour and process firmly into the forefront of political geographical analysis, thus contributing to shaking off the shackles of hitherto structure-orientated and descriptive based works. Jones' theory represents a framework within which the particular and unique can be applied in an orderly and clearly illustrated fashion. Its generic application is however limited by its universal inflexibility and oversimplification of complex political processes which have spatial consequences.

It was therefore becoming increasingly evident to many political geographers that more attention had to be paid to political behaviour and political processes. In order to make Political Geography explanatory, the new theoretical developments beginning to take shape in Political Science had to be taken into account. This desirability to progress from being merely a descriptive and chorological based sub-field of Geography, evoked debate between those who favoured an essentially geographical approach while an increasingly larger school argued for a desperate need to inject more politics into Political Geography. Hartshorne was relatively typical of the traditional school, consistently emphasising the need for a more geographical Political Geography. On the other hand, Jackson argued that political geographers would do well to pay less attention to geographical factors and consider the value of Politics when analysing spatio-political phenomena.[12] McColl proposed a middle of the road approach between Geography and Politics.[13] For him, the inter-relationships between political and geographical phenomena implied that, depending on the topic of research, it was necessary to vary emphasis, ranging on a spectrum from overtly geographical to overtly political considerations. In his proposed Political Ecology approach, both the politics behind geography and the converse, the geography behind politics, were acknowledged as valuable focuses for study. For example, for the former he advocated studying how politics affect the state's horizontal division while for the latter he suggested that political geographers could fruitfully examine the spatial distribution of phenomena and their relationships to political decisions and actions. However, the Political Ecology approach did nothing more than reaffirm the dilemma of what was Political Geography, restating the uncertainty shown by its practitioners as to exactly what uniquely concerned their discipline.

The avoidance of politics combined with the philosophy of excep-tionalism meant that Political Geography remained, characteristically, theory-deficient. Furthermore, just as Political Geography had failed to take note of developments in the maturing disciplines of Political Science and Political Sociology, a time-lag separated it from method-ological advances in mainstream Geography. Typical was its failure to latch on to what in effect became the mergence of the methodologies of logical positivism and neo-classical location theory, as brought in by the so called 'New Geography' of the late 1950s and 1960s. Quantifica-tion was of limited value to a subject whose theoretical roots were shallow and where its strength lay in idiographically-based and descrip-tive-orientated studies. Yet, at the same time, the new focus of the spatial analyst could hardly have facilitated the subject's revival. As Short puts it; 'The emphasis of neo-classical economics on the economy as a harmonious, self-regulating system, where each factor of produc-tion received its fair reward ignored questions of conflict and inequitable distribution and the focus of logical positivism directed attention to verifiable empirical statements in particular and data analysis in general and away from the more incorporeal power relations within society.'[14] This however did not prevent political geographers from somewhat belatedly succumbing to the fashion of the day; but instead of bringing the much awaited respectability to the subject, the adoption of quantitative tools and methods produced poorly tested, often naïve studies, which did little to raise its esteem. Ironically, this was at a time when the cognate discipline of Political Science was undergoing a retreat from poliometrics and similar numerical and statistical procedures.

More illuminating has been the utilisation of quantification in conjunction with a relatively well developed theoretical base, as typified in studies of administrative area reform and electoral geography. For example, Massam has analysed the influence of space and location on public service provision, focusing on the state's administrative areas and the optimal size for efficient functioning of local services, highlighting the inter-relationships between political and spatial organisations.[15] However by far the most successful and prolific employers of positivistic approaches have been researchers interested in elections. Building upon not only a relatively substantive geographical heritage, particularly in France, but also from voluminous sociological and political science contributions, political geographers have been active in examining the spatial variations in voting behaviour, the spatial influences on voting and the relationship within the political system between votes and how they are translated into seats based on constituency-areas.[16] Other quantitative studies considered the size and shape of states, particularly as they relate to a state's power,[17] and classifying international boundaries by measuring their temporal durability.[18]

For those political geographers conscious of the subject's political sterility, the generally held view amongst this growing school in the 1960s was that political systems modelling offered tremendous potential for integrating traditional perspectives in Political Geography with the ideas and methods of the political scientist. General systems theory appeared especially useful to writers such as Jackson, Cohen and Rosenthal, and Bergman who were interested in providing a holistic framework in which the interconnections between structure, process and behaviour could provide the organising principle to their studies.[19] The works of the political scientists, David Easton and Karl Deutsch, appeared particularly attractive. By considering the political organisation of the supra-state region, the state, and the urban metropolitan area as spatial systems, a number of aspects were considered. Soja, for example, measured the flows that affected connections within a supranational organisation by focusing on the probability of East African unity,[20] while Mackay considered the effectiveness of linguistic, cultural and political boundaries as barriers to social interaction.[21] Due recognition was also given to the political 'inputs' into the spatial system — in which studies acknowledged the 'demands' and 'supports' made by society and their eventual processing and sifting by government. It was however the political outcomes or 'outputs' in terms of spatial consequences which was to stimulate most research. For instance, the role of non-governmental actors (e.g. pressure groups, local communities) in influencing policy decisions has been taken up. Stephenson, for example, has considered ways of analysing the organisation and activities of pressure groups concerned with land-use and environmental issues by focusing primarily on how such conflicts are resolved through proposed land-use changes.[22]

Yet while the adoption of systems did open up important avenues for geographic enquiry, and in particular played a formative role in integrating the study of Electoral Geography into mainstream Political Geography by focusing on elections as 'feedback' through which demands and supports for the system are articulated, the spatial system was viewed as a system striving towards restoring equilibrium and maintenance of the *status quo*. As a consensus model of society, such an approach does not however reflect the real stuff of politics which is based on the principles underlying and the means by which particular groups acquire and hold onto a greater control over resources than others. By studying only balanced phenomena in a spatial system modelled as capable of functioning in a world in which social conflict and political disturbance can be resolved, the impression is given of systems always capable of restoring order. This has led Johnston, among others, to conclude that without a viable model for Political Geography that acknowledges conflict in society there can be little prospect of a Political Geography with politics.[23] To ignore the power of conflicting ideologies is to ignore the very ingredients of history.

How then are we to summarise the 'state of the art' at the end of the 1960s? Brian Berry had no doubt that it was a 'moribund backwater' because of its failure to come to grips with the geographer's newly found numeracy.[24] For others, the subject's lack of a conceptual dynamism compared with other sub-fields of Human Geography — particularly Economic and Urban Geography — was all too often mistakingly explained by ranking up *Geopolitik* as that age-old scapegoat for the subject's failings. Instead one must look to political geography's inability to develop a theoretical base which *integrates* space and politics. As Cohen and Rosenthal noted in 1971, 'Without more attention to the political, our geographical insights are likely to be limited and sterile.'[25] In part, lack of consideration of 'the political' is a product of lack of cross-fertilisation of ideas and concepts between Political Geography and its sister field, Political Science. Where such exchanges did occur they were unidirectional, with Political Geography borrowing from Political Science. But in general the political geographer did not greatly benefit from a discipline which itself had failed to produce adequate theory based on an overlap between spatial and political phenomena. Considerations of space generally played little more than an incidental role in explanation by political scientists. It is only recently that they have shown anything more than a casual treatment of geographical phenomena, hitherto usually viewed as relatively unimportant 'givens' in their political analysis. Kristof's 1960 statement that 'the bridge linking Geography and Politics must be built by and from both sides'[26] generally fell on stony ground. Thus in Political Science considerations of space added up to vague references to location, territory, physical environment and population distributions as background phenomena worthy only of cursory attention. This inability to borrow ready tailored ideas and models which could be adapted to a geographical perspective therefore put political geographers at a decided disadvantage compared with economic geographers who benefited from the economists' longstanding concern for distance, particularly when explaining industrial, agricultural and retail locations.

In the climate of heightened social awareness which has existed in Human Geography since the turn of the last decade, the human geographer, fully equipped with a wide range of positivist and behavioural approaches, considered such social welfare themes as poverty, housing, crime, social justice and policy making.[27] Such a change of emphasis in Human Geography, dubbed by Prince as concerned with 'social relevance',[28] involved liberal and neo-marxist geographers alike in formulating normative theories and new positivist approaches to such political issues. In the earlier stages of such a fundamental change in geographical thought, Political Geography appeared content to ponder over the value of quantification to their discipline,[29] an approach with which many human geographers had become dissatisfied because of its failure to explain the social problems of a complex and unequal society.[30]

Political Geography's inability to be at the forefront of geographical thought did little to raise its esteem in the eyes of many behavioural and radical human geographers. Indeed it has been suggested that its failure to become 'more political' has affected progress in Human Geography. As Archer has put it, 'A lagging Political Geography ... is a bottleneck to the advance of Human Geography generally.'[31]

RETHINKING POLITICAL GEOGRAPHY: SOMETHING OLD, SOMETHING NEW, SOMETHING BORROWED ...

We do not need to wait until the wise Owl of Minerva takes to the air before acknowledging that from the mid 1970s onwards, Political Geography has been in the process of undergoing something of a transformation. In Britain alone, since 1979, no less than six general textbooks, all novel in approach, have been published, more than outstripping the production rate of the previous decade.[32] Moreover, the launching in 1982 of *Political Geography Quarterly,* the first post-war journal of its kind, presents further evidence of a renewed interest in the subject. Inspired by recent trends in the social sciences, and, in particular, by the politicisation in approach of both Economic and Urban Geography, its rather overly sanguine editorial declared there to be every reason that 'at last, political geography's day has come.'[33]

Does all this mean that political geographers have cried wolf for the last time and that as Muir and Paddison have recently suggested, 'there are signs of it moving to occupy ... a more prominent position within human geography'?[34] While there is every indication to suggest that this is the case, it is certain that the rebirth of Political Geography has little to do with traditional approaches to the subject for its resurgence is primarily due to the belated importation of ideas based on Modern Political Economy, recent developments in Political Sociology, and critical social theory. It is the challenges that these approaches offer which mark the first serious attempt to inject politics into the subject. Yet, having said this, it would be shortsighted of contemporary political geographers to sever links with a rich empirical heritage, and, in particular, with works on the political region. Indeed, one of the tasks facing today's practitioners is to integrate the study of politics into their treatment of such regional organisations as supra-state alliances, the state, ethnic regions, and local government, and to establish the inter-relationships and connections within and between such spatio-political phenomena.

The Political Geography of the State

It is however fresh perspectives on the state which have gone furthest to revitalising Political Geography. In so far as the state is the most important form of spatio-political organisation in the modern world, it is not surprising that it has recently been singled out by geographers for special scrutiny. The concern with the advanced capitalist state in particular, especially the ways in which urban society has become increasingly under its shadow, has been approached from one of two lines of enquiry — liberal and Marxist — reflecting in these theories of the state the important part played by personal ideologies in both normative and descriptive analysis.

The liberal or welfare approach to the state has received most attention. The focus of this approach is based on an adapted version of Laswell's definition of Political Science as the study of 'who gets what, when and how in society',[35] recast in a spatial mould as 'who gets what, where'. Cox has considered at all scales in society what he identifies as the two main components of social well-being — residential quality and private income — and their relationships to locational choice, public policy and the juridical context.[36] Johnston has explored three determinants of the geography of social well-being — the spatial division of labour, governments and environments — and how, on the one hand, political and electoral systems and, on the other, social well-being, inter-relate with these political, social and spatial influences within the state.[37] In considering the politics of decision-making and its inter-relationships with spatial change, Muir and Paddison, while focusing primarily although not exclusively on the political system's outputs, have drawn attention to the political processes by which societies reallocate their unevenly distributed resources.[38]

This social welfare approach draws heavily upon Modern Political Economy. Here, economic concepts are applied to political events, the centrepiece of which is to view electoral votes as vital to understanding consumer choice and preference. This particular economic theory of democracy therefore takes the individual as the basic unit of analysis. One such line of enquiry believes in the existence of only minimal state intervention, based on the premise that individual values and ends are central and that the collective does not have a purpose which can be divorced from individual aims and objectives. Accordingly, Buchanan sees government as fulfilling two primary functions: first, it has a *protective role* to perform in which individual, voluntary exchange within a private market requires a degree of collective acknowledgement and perhaps enforcement of property rights; and secondly, it has a *productive role* to play where government acts as a device for producing goods and services when market transactions fail to deliver what individuals consider as necessary for their social welfare.[39] Following on from the Pareto-optimality criterion, one method used by economists as an efficiency gauge of a market economy, it is contended that only under specific circumstances can the state improve on the market and so regulate wealth distribution and individual choice in society. This is the field of the *geography of public goods*.[40] Public goods are defined as those goods and services available to all citizens, irrespective of location, where consumption by one individual does not reduce the amount available to others (e.g. state defence, clean air). This differs from impure public goods which are place-specific and which, due to variations in accessibility, are more available to some consumers than others (e.g. 999 services, public parks and other local amenities).

The non-excludability of a public good therefore means that it is impossible to prohibit someone from consuming a good or service without that individual paying for it. As it is argued that individuals have no incentive to reveal their preferences for a particular public good, its true demand is unknown and this leads to the underconsumption of a public good. This is referred to as the *freerider problem*. By way of an example, a city council provides a park for its residents, free of charge. This can have positive externality effects for daily commuters into the city who benefit from the facility but because they reside outside the council's jurisdiction, do not contribute via rates to its upkeep. They are the freeriders. Of course the argument can be countered by pointing to the fact that spending by commuters in the metropolitan area increases its prosperity, thereby compensating for the costs imposed on the city council and on some of the ratepayers.

The geographic literature on *public choice*[41] would challenge many of the above assumptions and state practices (particularly the use of taxes, subsidies), especially as any piece of collective (state) intervention can be introduced under the externality rubric. Their argument is that preventing, say, negative externalities through taxing producers who in their least cost method of production may impose social costs on a community, through, say, atmospheric pollution from an industrial plant, should be replaced by internalising externalities; that is by employing an appropriate legal-political framework. The problem of factory pollution would therefore be resolved through legal claims in which persons whose property was damaged would receive compensation. So in this brand of economic liberalism, the role of the state is primarily to implement a set of rules and regulations which govern property rights so that individuals can freely exchange with one another without imposing external costs. Such a method of intervention is seen to be more efficient than government action as public officials do not have the same incentive to be informed as private citizens.

Both public goods and public choice perspectives do however leave a number of important questions unanswered and some fields of enquiry untouched. Their political framework is based on the extent to which the activities of the advanced capitalist state has increasingly brought the individual under its shadow, while the geographical scale of enquiry focuses more or less exclusively at the urban level. So while this approach is to be commended for moving Political Geography in a more urban direction and thus taking note of developments in society in general, its neglect of the more macroscale, combined with its ahistorical view of the state, makes for a somewhat insular basis for reconstructing a Political Geography.

Critical of the Modern Political Economy approach are a number of alternative schools of thought which draw upon Marxist Political Economy and from critical social theory.[42] These approaches to the state often till a quite different soil but by doing so raise questions frequently overlooked by the Modern Political Economy literature. Rather than just simply asking 'who gets what, where in society', the line of enquiry here is also to ask questions of 'how' and 'why'. For instance, on the basis of the degree and method of intervention necessary by the state to maintain social order, Dear and Clark have identified various *functions* of the state, forming a basic framework for geographical study.[43] These include the following: firstly, as supplier of public goods, as regulator and facilitator of the operation of the market place, and as social engineer (in the sense of intervening in the economy to achieve state policy objectives); secondly, these three state functions are subsumed within the primary role of the state as 'arbiter' between competing social groups or classes; and finally, the state functions as 'agent' within society and the economy on behalf of a ruling class whose primary interest is to ensure the reproduction of the capitalist system. Approaches such as this have therefore located the political geography of the state within a capitalist world economy by illustrating ways in which the conduct of state decision-takers is both influenced and circumscribed by the dynamics of the global economic system. Thus, in effect, not only is the state examined *in* the international system but the international system is examined *in* the state. Moreover, such approaches also recognise that state activity is not just simply related to the productive and consumptive functions that it performs, but that the geography of human activity is also a product of other aspects of the state apparatus, most notably in connection with bureaucracy, law enforcement (police, military) and ideology (education, mass media).

It is not surprising given the empirical nature of much of current Political Geography that there is a microscale bias. This has led to much discussion and debate as to the nature and functions performed by the local state (or local government). Here a range of models and approaches have been used. On the one hand, most of the literature on the provision of public services provided by the local state have adopted a general liberal-pluralist standpoint. Bennett considers the primary function of the local state as providing necessary public services aimed at eradicating or at least reducing the unequal treatment of individuals in society with the aim of seeking to redistribute economic and social benefits.[44] Local government is therefore considered as facilitating as close a match as possible between variation in locational demand and response to demand. However, from a structural Marxist perspective, Clark argues that this is an unsatisfactory view of the local state for it sidesteps the crucial issue of the structural interdependency with, and control exercised by, a central state whose relationship in turn cannot be divorced from the dominant mode of production.[45] One cannot therefore assume that the local state is inherently democratic and egalitarian in nature for its actions and activities are circumscribed by the nature of the capitalist state. Yet as recent experience in Britain shows with regard to the Rate Support Grant, in which central government has at its disposal a political weapon that can be used to both penalise and reward local authorities, local government can often come into conflict with central directives over resource allocation and the management of services. Thus while Town Hall maybe unable to control local expenditures and allocate according to need, its existence at least provides a means for citizen participation and demand-making.

It is however not just central-local government relations which have generated an important focus for research but also the relationship between the state centre and its ethnic periphery. Despite conventional academic wisdom of the 1950s and 1960s that centre-periphery ethnic cleavages would be dissolved in the acid bath of modernity, the advanced capitalist state has failed to stem the tide of ethnic-based regional movements in such disparate societies and varying political systems as the United Kingdom, Spain, France, Canada and Belgium. Besides focusing on the reasons for the recent politicisation of such regional identities, a number of political geographers have considered their social formation and development as ethnic nations. Such explanations have focused on differential regional development, the role of linguistic and cultural markers, and the part played by the ethnic intelligentsia in politicising the socio-economic and political predicaments of their territorial communities.[46] Other investigations of ethnic nationalism have explored the relationships between the nation and various ideologies of national self-determination,[47] the scale of the nationalities problem in state socialist societies by drawing upon notions of adminstrative territorial control,[48] and the range of strategies and policies adopted by states (e.g. federalism, consociationalism, devolution) designed to resolve state-nation conflict.[49]

Geographical scale

Writing in the late 1960s, Kasperson and Minghi alleged that preoccupation with the state had tended to impede the theoretical development of Political Geography, a criticism directed primarily at the prominence given to geopolitical studies of the state.[50] It is somewhat paradoxical that today preoccupation with the state in relation to the urban-regional scale has been to the detriment of an international focus. No major work on the geopolitics of the global arena has been published since Cohen's 1973 revised text on *Geography and Politics in a World Divided*,[51] although topics such as the International Law of the Sea,[52] and frontier studies still receive ample consideration. Belatedly, however, the importance of developing a geography of East-West relations is being taken up as political geographers take note that conflicts between central and local government, between capital and labour, and between nation and state, pale into insignificance when due recognition is given to the context and stakes within which interstate conflict is being conducted.[53] Thus one of the most socially useful aspects of applied Political Geography to emerge in recent years concerns the likely spatial impacts of nuclear attack, with the intention that such findings should be used in public debate to inform both the authorities and the public of likely consequences based on a number of probable scenarios.[54] Cohen has also drawn attention to the scope for geopolitical remodelling by drawing upon the developmental approach in general systems theory.[55] By so doing he illustrates how the geopolitical map is evolving into one of hierarchical integration in which two levels are crucial — superpower globalism and regional or second-order powers. In a similar vein, O'Laughlin has attempted to synthesise traditional geostrategic approaches with recent quantitative perspectives on the international relations literature in an attempt to develop geographic models of international conflicts.[56] The importance of the East-West co-ordinate in international relations is also taken up in a refreshingly different way by Agnew who focuses on how a superpower like the United States legitimises its policies of 'expansion' and 'containment' in the name of the country's *unique* character, a practice which can be traced back to the importance of the frontier in American history.[57] Such an approach, however, should be considered in conjunction with a world economy perspective in which superpower behaviour is contextualised in terms of competitive state actions.

Yet while research in Political Geography is developing on a more balanced footage when considered in relation to its three fold scale-division — the international, state, and local levels — it is only recently that its practitioners have acknowledged that such *distinct* political geographic levels of enquiry are counter to an *integrated* Political Geography. As Taylor has noted, "With such disparate themes as the 'distribution of urban public goods' and 'geostrategy in the nuclear era' it is not surprising that these scales became seen as distinct and separate."[58] His suggestion of locating Political Geography within the holistic approach of a materialist (and thus global) framework has therefore many advantages.[59] After all, how can we consider the all too often subtle inter-relationships of society and economy with politics as purely internal to the state? Surely to do so is to ignore the complexities of political processes and the way in which the world economy impacts upon the conduct, nature and dynamics of the state and internal political activity. What he identifies are three *inter-connected* geographic scales — the world economy as the scale of reality, the state representing the scale of ideology, and the city as the scale of experience. Provided that one acknowledges the limitations of such a scheme — particularly claims that the advanced capitalist state has internal political domination but exists in an international environment in which economic mechanisms hold sway, that a cultural and political phenomenon such as nationalism is simply a reaction to economic dominance, and that the state socialist world can be neatly considered as a variant of the capitalist state — then this framework is a valuable basis for investigating a number of themes in Political Geography.

CONCLUSIONS: TOWARDS A POLITICAL GEOGRAPHY OF POWER RELATIONS

In contrast to the subject's hazy recent past, Political Geography is in the throws of being recognised as a vital and indeed more central field of study in geographic research. Political scientists and political sociologists are also recognising that space is important in understanding the constitution of politics and society, and this has greatly stimulated Political Geography. Even so, major problems still remain. Most fundamental is the lack of clarity shown by its practitioners as to what the basis of Political Geography should be. This is most clearly reflected in *Political Geography Quarterly*'s first editorial in which no less than twenty-one themes are outlined as part of the subject's research agenda for the 1980s.[60] The alarming aspect is their tripartite division into 'geographical themes', 'geographical perspectives', and 'methodology and theory', implying, first, that somehow theory and method can be detached from empirical research, and second, that Political Geography can be neatly divided on the bases of 'the geography behind politics' (geographical themes) and 'the politics behind geography' (geographical perspectives), reminiscent of the type of superficial and misleading modes of explanation put forward by the *political ecology* approach of the fifties. Until political geographers view space as embedded in and undetachable from society and thus politics, then there can be little prospect of future advances in the subject.

Moreover, as the last two sections illustrate, the subject matter of Political Geography is wide-ranging. This should be its strength, not its weakness, for to consider the arena of Political Geography as simply 'who gets what, where' in relation to government is to view politics as simply the domain and activity of government. In defining Political Geography as 'the study of those economic and social conflicts which focus on the state and which have clear spatial and/or environmental components'[61] Johnston offers a more dynamic and broader conception of what is politics but even here it is the state and not politics which is considered as the kernel of Political Geography. According to this viewpoint, there can be no politics without focusing on the state. Thus to give an extreme example, we would have to conclude, unsatisfactorally, that in primitive societies where the state plays little or no role in organising human activity there is no politics and no Political Geography to investigate.

What I am therefore arguing is that the focus of Political Geography should be politics. In this regard, politics must be viewed as both a *process* and a *universal activity,* in which we are primarily concerned with power relations in space at all levels and scales in the political hierarchy, including both formal and informal group activity. As Claval suggests, a Political Geography which begins to think in terms of developing a spatial theory of the exercise of power would provide a more coherent Political Geography, for 'power, authority and influence are consubstantial aspects of all social life within a defined area: they stem from the unequal distribution of resources, the existence of strategic positions, advantages conferred by transport and communication services and all types of exchange.'[62] Thus power is about space; about those processes and activities which influence and reflect the *management* and *distribution* of power in space; and about the consequences of this for resource use and distribution; it is about the capacity of various social agents to influence change. It is therefore to do with economy, with social structure, and with culture, and not just government activity. Such a broadly conceived view stresses the inherently interdisciplinary nature of the subject of politics which is, as Held and Leftwich call, 'the lived interdisciplinarity of all collective social life.'[63] If Political Geography were to develop along this path then we are more likely to secure a bridge between it and the rest of the Political Sciences which is not simply represented by a number of narrow and underutilised positions but rather by a unified and bustling freeway.

144

● NOTES

1. F. Ratzel: Politische Geographie (Munich: Oldenbourg, 1897).

2. H. J. Mackinder, 'The Geographical Pivot of History', Geogr. J., 23 (1904), 421 ff.

3. H. J. Mackinder: Democratic Ideals and Reality (New York: Constable, 1919).

4. I. Bowman: The New World (London: Harrap, 1921).

5. C. B. Fawcett: The Provinces of England (1919) (London: Hutchinson revised edition, 1961).

6. See, A. Gyorgy: Geopolitics: The New German Science (Berkeley: University of California Press, 1944).

7. Quoted in H. H. Sprout, 'Geopolitical hypotheses in technological perspective', World Politics, 15 (1963), 190-1.

8. R. Hartshorne, 'The Functional Approach in Political Geography', Ann.Ass.Amer.Geogr., XI (1950), 95-130.

9. Ibid.

10. J. Gottmann, 'The Political Partitioning of Our World: An Attempt at Analysis', World Politics, IV (1952), 512-9.

11. S. Jones, 'A Unified Field Theory of Political Geography', Ann.Ass. Amer.Geogr., 44 (1954), 111-23.

12. W. A. D. Jackson, 'Whither Political Geography?', Ann.Ass.Amer.Geogr., 48 (1958), 178-83.

13. R. W. McColl, 'Political Geography as Political Ecology', The Professional Geogr., 18 (1966), 143-5.

14. J. Short: An Introduction to Political Geography (London: Routledge and Kegan Paul, 1982).

15. B. Massam: Location and Space in Social Administration (London: Edward Arnold, 1975).

16. The range of quantitative approaches to electoral geography is considerable. For comprehensive bibliographies see: P. J. Taylor and R. J. Johnston: Geography of Elections (Harmondsworth: Penguin, 1979); G. Gudgin and P. J. Taylor: Seats, Votes and the Spatial Organisation of Elections (London: Pion, 1978).

17. R. Muir: Modern Political Geography (London: Macmillan, 1975), 51-57; G. East and J. R. V. Prescott: Our Fragmented World. An Introduction to Political Geography (London: Macmillan, 1975), 55-63.

18. A. Learmonth and C. Hamnett: Approaches to Political Geography (Bletchley: Open University Press, 1971), 28-32.

19. S. B. Cohen and D. Rosenthal, 'A Geographical Model for Political Systems Analysis', Geogr.Rev., 61 (1971), 5-31; E. Bergman: Modern Political Geography (Dubuque: Wm. C. Brown, 1975); W. A. D. Jackson: Politics and Geographic Relationships (Englewood Cliffs, N.J.: Prentice Hall, 1964).

20. E. Soja, 'Communications and Territorial Integration in East Africa: An Introduction to Transaction Flow Analysis', East Lakes Geogr., 4 (1968), 39-57.

21. J. R. Mackay, 'The Interactance Hypothesis and Boundaries in Canada', Canadian Geogr., 11 (1958), 1-8.

145

22. L. K. Stephenson, 'Toward Spatial Understanding of Environmentally-Based Voluntary Groups', Geoforum, 10 (1979), 195-201.

23. R. J. Johnston, 'Political Geography without Politics', Prog.in Hum. Geogr., 4 (1980), 439-46.

24. B. Berry, in a review of B. M. Russett's International Regions and the International System: A Study in Political Ecology, Geogr.Rev., LIX (1969), 450.

25. S. B. Cohen and D. Rosenthal, (1971), op.cit., 6.

26. L. D. K. Kristof, 'The origins and evolution of geopolitics', J. of Conflict Resolution, 4 (1960), 33.

27. Some of the earlier and more influential contributions included; D. Harvey: Social Justice and the City (London: Edward Arnold, 1973); D. M. Smith: Human Geography: a welfare approach (London: Edward Arnold, 1977); R. Peet (ed.): Geography of American Poverty, Special issue of Antipode 2 (Worcester, 1970); H. M. Rose: The Black Ghetto: A Spatial Behavioural Perspective (New York: McGraw-Hill, 1971); R. Peet (ed.): Radical Geography: alternative viewpoints on contemporary social issues (London: Methuen, 1977). In addition, human geographers debated 'Geography and Public Policy' in a number of articles published in Inst.Brit.Geogr.Transactions, no. 63, (1974) 1-52.

28. H. Prince, 'Questions of Social Relevance', Area, 3 (1971), 150-3.

29. R. D. Dikshit, 'The retreat from political geography', Area, 9 (1977), 234-9.

30. F. Walsh, 'Time-lag in political geography', Area, 11 (1979), 91-2.

31. J. C. Archer, 'Political Geography', Prog.in Hum.Geogr., 4 (1980), 256.

32. A. Burnett and P. Taylor: Political Studies from Spatial Perspectives (Chichester: Wiley, 1981); R. Johnston: Political, Electoral and Spatial Systems (London: Clarendon, 1979); R. Johnston: Geography and the State. An Essay in Political Geography (London: Macmillan, 1982); R. Muir and R. Paddison: Politics, Geography and Behaviour (London: Methuen, 1981); R. Paddison: The Fragmented State: The Political Geography of Power (Oxford: Blackwell, 1983); J. Short: An Introduction to Political Geography (London: Routledge and Kegan Paul, 1982).

33. Editorial, Political Geography Quarterly 1 (1), 1982, 1.

34. R. Muir and R. Paddison (1981), op.cit., 7.

35. H. D. Lasswell: Politics: Who gets What, When and How (Cleveland: World Publishing Co., 1958).

36. K. R. Cox: Location and Public Problems: A Political Geography of the Contemporary World (Oxford: Blackwell, 1979).

37. R. J. Johnston (1979), op.cit.

38. R. Muir and R. Paddison (1981), op.cit.

39. J. Buchanan: The Limits of Liberty (Chicago, 1975).

40. See, for example, R. J. Bennett: The Geography of Public Finance (London: Methuen, 1980); A. C. Lea 'Welfare theory, public goods and public facility location', Geographical Analysis, 1979, 11, 217-39.

41. See, for example, D. R. Reynolds, 'The geography of social choice', in Burnett and Taylor (1981), op.cit., 91-109.

146

42. See, for example, G. Clark and M. Dear: State Apparatus (Boston: Allen and Unwin, 1984); R. Johnston: Geography and the State. An Essay in Political Geography (London: Macmillan, 1982); J. Short: An Introduction to Political Geography (London: Routledge and Kegan Paul, 1982), G. E. Smith, 'Political Geography, Politics and the State', Social Sciences Research Journal 1983, 8 (3), 30-56.

43. M. Dear and G. Clark, 'The State and Geographic Process: a critical review', Environment and Planning A, 1978, 10, 173-83.

44. R. J. Bennett, 1980, op.cit.

45. G. Clark, 'Democracy and the Capitalist State: towards a critique of the Trebout hypothesis', in Burnett and Taylor (1981), op.cit., 111-30.

46. See, for example, J. Agnew, 'Structural and Dialectical Theories of Political Regionalism', in Burnett and Taylor, 1981, op.cit., 275-89; D. Fitzpatrick, 'The geography of Irish Nationalism, 1910-21', Past and Present, 1978, 78, 113-44; G. E. Smith, 'Nationalism, Regionalism and the State', 1985, 3 (1), 3-9; C. H. Williams, 'Ethnic Resurgence in the Periphery', Area, 1979, 11 (4), 279-83.

47. D. Knight, 'Identity and Territory: Geographical Perspectives on Nationalism and Regionalism', Annals Assoc. of American Geogr. 1982, 72, 514-31; D. Knight, 'Self-Determination as a Geopolitical Force', J. of Geography, 1983, 82, 148-52.

48. G. E. Smith, 'Ethnic Nationalism in the Soviet Union: Territory, Cleavage and Control', Environment and Planning C. Government and Policy, 1985, 3 (1).

49. E. Kofman, 'Regional Autonomy and the One and Indivisible French Republic', Environment and Planning C. Government and Policy, 1985, 3 (1), 11-26; C. H. Williams, 'When Nationalists Challenge: When Nationalists Rule', Environment and Planning C. Government and Policy, 1985, 3 (1), 27-48.

50. R. Kasperson and J. Minghi (eds.): The Structure of Political Geography (Chicago: Aldine, 1969), 12.

51. S. B. Cohen, Geography and Politics in a World Divided 2nd edit. (New York: OUP, 1973).

52. See J. R. V. Prescott: The Political Geography of the Oceans (London: David & Charles, 1975); A. D. Couper: The Law of the Sea (London: Macmillan, 1978); R. D. Hodgson and R. W. Smith, 'Boundary Issues Created by Extended National Marine Jurisdiction', Geogr.Rev., 69 (1979), no. 4; R. W. Smith, 'Trends in National Maritime Claims', Prof.Geogr., 32 (1980), no. 2.

53. For example, A. Jenkins, 'Territorial issues in the Sino-Soviet Conflict', Tijdschrift voor Econ.en.Soc.Geografie, 65 (1974); M. Glassner, 'The Bedouin of Southern Sinai under Israel Administration', Geogr.Rev., 64 (1974); H. Salisbury, 'The Israeli-Syrian Demilitarized Zone: An Example of Unresolved Conflict', J.of Geogr., 71 (1972), 109-16; J. W. House, 'Frontier Studies: an applied approach', in Burnett and Taylor, (1981), op.cit., 291-312.

54. See, for example, S. Openshaw and P. Steadman, 'The geography of two hypothetical nuclear attacks in Britain', Area, 15, 1983, 193-201; D. Pepper and A. Jenkins, 'A call to arms: geography and peace studies', Area, 15, 1983, 202-8.

55. S. B. Cohen, 'A New Map of Global Geopolitical Equilibrium: A Developmental Approach', Political Geography Quarterly, 1982, 1, 223-42.

56. J. O'Loughlin, 'Geographic Models in International Conflicts', in P. Taylor and J. House, 1984, op.cit., 202-16.

57. J. Agnew, 'An Excess of "National Exceptionalism": Towards A New Political Geography of American Foreign Policy', Political Geography Quarterly, 1983, 2 (2), 151-66.

58. P. Taylor, 'Geographical Scale and Political Geography', in Taylor and House, (1984), op.cit., 3.

59. P. Taylor, A Materialist Framework for Political Geography, Transactions, Institute of British Geographers, 7, 15-34.

60. Editorial, (1982), op.cit.

61. R. J. Johnston, (1980), op.cit., 440.

62. P. Claval, 'The Coherence of Political Geography: Perspectives on its Past Evolution and its Future Relevance', in P. Taylor and J. House, (1984), op.cit., 21.

63. D. Held and A. Leftwich, 'A Discipline of Politics?', in A. Leftwich, ed.: What is Politics? Its Activity and Its Study (Oxford: Blackwell, 1984), 143.

SELECT BIBLIOGRAPHY

A. Burnett and P. Taylor (eds.): Political Studies from Spatial Perspectives (Chichester: Wiley, 1981).

G. Clark and M. Dear: State Apparatus (Boston: Allen and Unwin, 1984).

K. R. Cox: Location and Public Problems. A Political Geography of the Contemporary World (Oxford: Blackwell, 1979).

J. Gottman (ed.): Centre and Periphery: Spatial variations in Politics (London: Sage, 1980).

R. Johnston: Geography and the State. An Essay in Political Geography (London: Macmillan, 1982).

R. Muir: Modern Political Geography (London: Macmillan, 1981).

R. Paddison: The Fragmented State: The Political Geography of Power (Oxford: Blackwell, 1983).

J. Short: An Introduction to Political Geography (London: Routledge and Kegan Paul, 1982).

P. Taylor and J. House (eds.): Political Geography. Recent Advances and Future Directions (London: Croom Helm, 1984).

Development Studies

Neil Casey and Alex Cunliffe

Across the social sciences the last twenty years has witnessed Development Studies jostling its way onto curricula all over the education system. Within degree structures individual disciplines have increasingly given space to courses and sections with such titles as Comparative Political Development, the Sociology of Development and Economic Development. Moreover, this period has seen, what can collectively be called Development Studies experiencing a rapid, profound and academically stimulating adolescence. Initially it was overly concerned with abstracted notions of change and merely extending the realms of traditional, comparative Political Science and Sociology. Gradually, though, the subject has focused on the highly pertinent matters — given, for instance, the world banking crisis and the Brandt Report, let alone the levels of human suffering involved — of modern development and the nature of Third World societies.

This paper will provide an overview of the development of Development Studies. Preliminarily we shall trace the focus, parameters and characteristics of the burgeoning study of development. It is then our intention to describe the often diverse theoretical perspectives adopted by Political Science and Sociology to confront the subjects' central issues. Finally we shall assess both the intellectual problems and difficulties that the study of development has encouraged and revealed, and its not inconsiderable academic achievements.

THE RISE OF DEVELOPMENT STUDIES

The emergence of Development Studies reflects the unfolding of a fundamental, global problem. This is the crystallisation of a recognisable Third World comprised of nation states exhibiting an undoubtedly different and, relative to the standards of the First World of the advanced capitalist countries and Second World of the Soviet bloc nations, significantly 'lower' level of development. Economic weakness, political instability, excessive bureaucracy, poverty and disease and alien (for the Western social scientist) cultural mores are just some of our stereotyped but nevertheless generally realistic images of Third World societies.

The growing awareness and persistence of a development gap in conjunction with the 'novelty' of Third World societies — particularly with regard to their modes of development — posed the political scientists and sociologists of the liberal democracies some quite basic questions. In the search for answers, broadly speaking, two dominant and contrasting approaches appeared throughout the social science disciplines. Encamped at one end of the ideological spectrum is modernisation theory. It grew out of American structural-functionalism and essentially sees development occurring along a universal continuum of evolution. The social and political peak of this continuum is a modern industrialised, democratic society resembling the advanced Western nations. At the other end is a radical theoretical response with the common assumption that the Third World has been structurally deformed to its disadvantage by the First World's imposition of colonialism and international capitalism.[1]

In dealing with fundamental issues, then, Development Studies, as we shall relate in more detail, has been dominated by these two distinct perspectives. The most obvious question to be tackled is why a development gap between the First and Third Worlds — and such a wide gap — should have occurred? Does the explanation lie, as modernisation theory would have it, in the fact that 'traditional' Third World societies are hindered by the absence of the requisite, modern institutions and values and a 'development ethic'? Or is it the case that the advanced capitalist nations have historically manufactured a gap by retarding the rest of the world for their own aggrandisement? This latter theory is, of course, rooted ultimately in Marx's conception of capitalist expansion and the work of Lenin, Luxemburg and others on imperialism.[2] Contention between the two schools of thought here is revealed terminologically by the use of on the one hand 'developing' or 'undeveloped' and on the other 'underdeveloped' to describe Third World nations.

A related next question revolves around the influences, causes and, for some, determinants of development. More precisely it considers how the Third World should *now* develop. Modernisation theory holds that the 'developing' nations require a diffusion of the institutions and values which enabled the *capitalist,* liberal democracies to develop into their modern forms. The radical or neo-Marxist perspective includes devotees of a structural break from the inhibiting force of the capitalist world system. To replace it there should be an independent *socialist* society within a socialist world economy. The adoption of these polar, ideological positions once again reflects recent history with Third World societies tending to pursue paths of internal development within a capitalist or socialist orbit.

These kinds of considerations eventually required that development theorists stand back and give some thought to the apparently common-sensical issue of the reality of development itself. What is development? Modernisation theorists, in the main, have seen it as a progression towards what Rostow called "the age of high mass consumption";[3] their vision is based on the model of the modern, industrialised, capitalist societies.[4] The advent of various socialist revolutions, however, has led radical observers to condemn a definition of development which, for them, smacks of Western academic arrogance. The Chinese and Cuban revolutions, for instance, apart from proclaiming the possibilities of alternative social systems, queried the centrality of industrialisation, democracy and market mechanisms in definitions of development.

Thus, world events had demanded that social scientists begrudgingly dispense with their intellectual assumptions based on the study of the liberal democracies. In actuality, this unhealthy parochialism had left them bereft of analytical tools with which to understand 20th century development, the development gap, and the specific nature of Third World societies. However, from this myopic beginning, development theorists further undermined themselves by donning disciplinary blinkers.[5] It seemed, and still does to some extent, that the separate disciplines of Political Science, Sociology, Economics, History and Anthropology, were operating in splendid isolation. Each set about dealing with the 'problem of development' from its own disciplinary base.

The degree to which the study of development has forced the separate disciplines to escape what sometimes seem like administrative boundaries — a process suggested by the appearance *throughout* the social sciences of the two prevailing perspectives — will be one of the issues explored later. As such it constitutes a core aspect of the advance of development theory within the social sciences.

THEORETICAL DEVELOPMENTS IN DEVELOPMENT THEORY

A close historiographical analysis of the study of development within Political Science and Sociology reveals both the academic specialisation within the social sciences and the emergence of common theoretical threads. It can be seen also that this theoretical activity falls into a number of distinct post-Second World War phases.[6] The first phase, based primarily amidst the large scale decolonisation process of the 1950s and early 1960s, seemed to be concerned with the horizons facing these newly independent states. Inevitably perhaps, within a Western intellectual environment which seemed anxious both to write the funeral oration of fascism and downgrade the Stalinist panacea of communism[7] the social social science community at this time operated within a functionalist framework. This implicitly concentrated upon the eminent suitability of liberal democratic political institutions and what was basically a capitalist social system for the Third World.

The second stage, approximately encompassing a decade from the early 1960s, reflected growing academic disillusionment with the suitability of such liberal democratic-capitalist models. With the realisation that the liberal democratic quasi-capitalist inheritance passed onto the post-colonial state may be neither a realistic nor desirable long term prospect, a large division appeared in the approach towards Development Studies. On the one hand, a number of writers, largely retaining their ethnocentric approach, chose to redefine and reassess the goals that could be reasonably expected from Third World systems. On the other hand, a number of academics, notably A. G. Frank, introduced a radical perception of the political, social and economic demise of the Third World under a thesis which was to be labelled 'dependency theory' and which was to act as a catalyst for a new approach in the Development Studies debate. Indeed, the third phase in the academic analysis of Third World societies, dating from the mid-1970s, has witnessed a re-evaluation of dependency theory and the appearance of explanations for 'underdevelopment' which have their place on both the Left and Right of the political spectrum.

Here then are three phases in the treatment of Development Studies which emphasise the aforementioned theoretical and ideological divisions. If we are to understand the concept of development in any detail, each of these stages both in Political Science and Sociology needs to be investigated more fully.

First Phase

The combined intellectual heritage of, the failure of fascism, the appalling human rights record of Stalinist Russia, and the perceived economic successes of Western industrialised democracy, all served to encourage many social scientists to develop *functionalist,* liberal democratic models for the newly independent states of the Third World. Common to these models is the idea of a universal route of societal evolution so that *all* societies exist somewhere on a development scale. The stimulus for this approach came from Sociology and particularly Talcott Parsons. In his work and that of sociologists such as Hagen and Eisenstadt, development was analysed with regard to a society's functional specialisation.[8] Generally speaking a society is more advanced the greater its stage of social differentiation. For these theorists the USA epitomised modernity and the Third World exemplified simpler traditional societies.

Political development could be measured, to provide one example, by a nation's relative possession of such political qualities as 'institutionalisation', 'differentiation', 'integration' and 'legitimacy'. As these traits would suggest, liberal democracies could be located at the upper end of the evolutionary ladder whilst the Third World languished far below. This liberal democratic approach is implicitly, even explicitly, expressed in the work of Apter in his specific study of Ghanaian politics and in the more general, development studies of Almond and Coleman and Almond and Verba.[9]

For both Political Science and Sociology the solution to the Third World's alleged traditionality lay in the diffusion of the necessary political, social, cultural and economic institutions and values. However, the ethnocentric, ideological character of these studies, perhaps encapsulated most vividly by Rostow in his metaphoric vision of underdeveloped societies as aeroplanes about to 'take-off' into the levels of growth enjoyed by Western, capitalist democracies, did not coincide with the political, social and economic realities of the Third World. Indeed, from 1965, a number of empirical studies began to emphasise the inappropriate and unacceptable nature of the liberal democratic-capitalist inheritance for many parts of the post colonial world.[10] As a result there was to be a steady but distinct transformation in the academic approach to development studies.

Second Phase

As the 1960s progressed, a number of political scientists chose to redirect the nature of Development Studies by redefining political development in terms of 'order' rather than 'democracy'. Zolberg and Huntington were notable at this time amongst those academics who interpreted development and 'modernisation' in terms of a system's ability to suppress the strains of social mobilisation and political participation.[11] Essentially, however, the character of such studies did not run counter to the problematic functionalist perspective of the earlier phase. Furthermore, by continuing on this theoretical path they ignored the failure of modernisation theory to practically mobilise Third World Development, and the fact that having experienced revolutions, various societies were undergoing accelerated development in isolation from the capitalist world system.

The inevitable challenge to modernisation theory came from a neo-Marxist critique and most notably from A. G. Frank. He provided a seemingly more viable explanation *and* coaxed Development Studies out of its disciplinary atomisation by stressing the necessity for economic and historical analysis.[12] He accused his predecessors in Development Studies of being little more than apologists for neo-colonialism and he intrinsically challenged their assumption that underdevelopment was an original condition over which international capitalism held little influence. In the ensuing debate, a number of related, radical critiques gained prominence and, with the label of 'dependency theorists', they demonstrated the ways in which capitalist penetration had underdeveloped the Third World.[13] At the core of dependency theory is the idea that, in Frank's words " . . . it is capitalism, both world and national, which produced underdevelopment in the past and which still generates underdevelopment in the present."[14] The advanced nations, then, within the capitalist structure of colonialism engaged in first plunder, and then 'exploitation'. The vagueness of this latter concept led Arghiri Emmanuel and Samir Amin to subsequently refine the analysis with the idea of 'unequal exchange'.[15] Basically this refers to the relationship within which the Third World is forced to sell its raw materials cheaply and buy First World manufactures expensively. Common to the analyses in their revelation of a vast, continuing outflow of capital from what have become under-developed societies back to the developed world. The result for the Third World is a deformed and debilitated society totally oriented to and *dependent* upon the aims and vicissitude of the dominant society (Frank calls them satellite and metropolis). *Independent* development will only be achieved through revolutionary activity and a structural split from international capitalism.

Within this Frank-inspired interdisciplinary genre was a growing number of development studies which began to consider 'political instutitons' prevalent in the Third World — for example military governments and single party systems — in terms of mainstream 'sociological' concepts such as class, bureaucracy and the state.[16] Thus, Frank and the others had not only delivered a damning critique of what passed for orthodoxy in Development Studies and provided a credible, radical alternative, but also had shaken many scholars out of their disciplinary isolation.

Third Phase

However, some remained entrenched in singular conservatism. From 1971, the non-Marxist academic approach to the notion of 'political development' retained the preoccupation with the maintenance of order but also began to emphasise governmental capacity to introduce public policy. Thus, starting perhaps with Binder *et al.* and Apter the study of development acquired a rational-choice, public policy character in which a gradual and evolutionary process of change was advocated.[17] This refinement was later encompassed in the work of Rothstein and, notably, in a revised edition of Almond and Powell's *Comparative Politics* which was appropriately re-subtitled, 'System, Process and Policy'.[18] This approach has found extensions both in the liberal recommendations of the Brandt Report and, further to the Right, with P. Bauer who expresses the belief that 'development' can only be achieved via a slow moving, indigenous process which must be *internally* nurtured rather than instantly created with the external funding of foreign aid.[19] In this respect he shares with many neo-Marxists a contempt for the advanced capitalist world's proclaimed interest in, and practical help, for the Third World.

Radical studies of development from the early 1970s can primarily be seen as an attempt to refine or even overturn some of the generalisations and deficiencies of the earlier 'Frankian' dependency theorists. A number of writers, notably Warren and Cardoso questioned the assertions that capitalism invariably *caused* underdevelopment, or that Third World stagnation was universally the outcome of an international capitalist environment.[20] Prominent amongst those who, like Amin and Emmanuel, have attempted to sophisticate Frank is Immanuel Wallerstein, the architect of World Systems Theory.[21] For Wallerstein the developmental unit of analysis should be the world capitalist system in which *all* modern states participate through exchange for profit. Inequality between the First and Third Worlds is determined by the relative strength of state mechanisms which allow certain states to impose on others an exploitative system of capital exchange.

However, dependency theory and World System Theory has been the target of heated disagreement from orthodox Marxists or 'productionists'.[22] Laclau was one of those who demanded a return to a 'purer' Marxist analysis taking into account modes of production and class analysis.[23] He denied the existence of one, global mode of production claiming that Third World societies, for instance, possessed several side by side. Only through the analysis of individual societies' modes of production could development be comprehended and thus influenced. As evidence Marxists have pointed to the history of the 'socialist' societies which shows that development has occurred not primarily through acquiring a bigger share of an existing world surplus (as 'circulationists' would have it), but by changing the internal class structure.

There have been, though, attempts at synthesis. Banaji has argued that whilst different modes of production exist there is a *dominant* mode of production. In the modern world this is invariably capitalist and its dominance will enable it to affect all political and social institutions resulting, for example in *capitalist* underdeveloped societies.[24] The wider complex of relations between classes and states in *different* societies has been emphasised by Petras. He points out that capitalist expansion originally promoted the creation of collaborative classes in the Third World and they helped exploit labour internally and orient production towards the imperial power.[25]

Thus, in recent years there has been a lively dialogue within and between conservative and radical schools of Development Studies, particularly with regard, on the one hand, to the use of aid, and on the other, the role of international capital and the nature of class formation in the post-colonial state.[26] The debate's animation and rapid change is an indication of both the urgent relevancy of the subject matter and the invigorating effect it has had on the social sciences.

PROGRESSIONS, PROBLEMS AND PRESCRIPTIONS?

In a relatively short time Development Studies has covered a remarkable amount of intellectual ground. As Cohen has remarked, the study of development is responsible for the resurgence of a broad comparative perspective.[27] Despite the early parochialism entailed in applying liberal democratic and capitalist models to the Third World, Development Studies has supplied an extra analytic dimension simply through the examination of a greater number of varied societies. Implicit here is a shift away from a haughty ethnocentricity. Although uncommon in other parts of the educational system, the study of a global problem has, often through the efforts of Third World scholars, begun the assembly of a global and globally-minded academic community.

Development Studies has also managed to provoke a progressive, vigorous debate, particularly within Sociology and Political Science. In its brief lifetime it has jolted the complacency of structural-functionalists, encouraging both them and Marxists to reinvestigate their foundations. The neo-Marxist entry into the fray was an important advance for its reincarnation of the historical, economic, 'total' approach common to both 'circulationists' and 'productionists'.

However, the study of development is still constrained. Specifically, it is hampered by its admittedly reduced but nevertheless persistent *disciplinary specialisation* and by an *ethnocentricity* outside the subject area which leaves students insufficiently armed when dealing with the decidedly international matter of development.

Despite the trend away from disciplinary isolation started by the radical critique of modernisation theory there is still a tendency, conspicuous within Political Science, to confine analysis to what are viewed as strictly disciplinary problems. Often though, the work of political scientists and sociologists, for instance, seem to be different aspects of a *common* development process. The potential waste of replicated resources and teaching is exemplified by text books. To provide one instance, Higgott's *Political Development Theory* and Hoogvelt's *The Sociology of Developing Societies* cover a great deal of shared ground.[28]

Wasteful replication is one possible result; an 'incomplete' analysis is another. The very fact that the same two prevailing perspectives have been operative across the social sciences points to the similarity and inextricable relation of the objects of scrutiny. 'Development' is an intrinsically holistic and *multi-disciplinary* phenomenon. Its study is dangerously weakened by limitation to, for example, a political problem without a socio-economic and historical dimension. Accordingly we would agree with those who argue for a unified, and hence more realistic approach to development. One possibility is the inauguration of further integrated 'development' courses such as the

Open University's *Third World Studies.*[29]

Development Studies is also hindered by the general insularity of British educational culture. Although it has, by dint of its very subject matter engendered a global awareness amongst its theorists this has not been reproduced amongst many students. The fault lies not with the subject, nor with the students but with an educational universe which has *British* social and political life at its *centre.*[30] Whilst social science pupils are educationally weaned on such components as '*British* Constitution', 'the sociology of modern *Britain*' and 'macro-economic analysis of postwar *Britain*', they will come ill-equipped for the diversity of world development. They will continue to be unable to contribute to or advance the critical study of development. Consequently it should be the responsibility of the social science establishment to find methods of generating a global awareness and global understanding of a global question. Development Studies would not be the only beneficiary.

● NOTES

1. We acknowledge the divergence within 'radical' Development Studies but feel justified in grouping disparate orientations together on the grounds of a common intellectual debt to Marx. See A. Foster-Carter, 'Neo-Marxist Approaches to Development and Underdevelopment', in E. De Kadt and G. Williams (eds.): Sociology and Development (London: Tavistock, 1974).

2. See A. Brewer: Marxist Theories of Imperialism (London: Routledge and Kegan Paul, 1982).

3. W. W. Rostow: The Stages of Economic Growth — A Non-Communist Manifesto (Cambridge: Cambridge University Press, 1960).

4. One line of thought viewed development as a 'convergence' between capitalism and socialism culminating in post-industrial society. D. Bell: The End of Ideology (New York: Free Press, 1965).

5. The dangers of continuing disciplinary specialisation are considered in the course of the article. See also R. A. Higgott: Political Development Theory (London: Croom Helm, 1983).

6. For further historiographical analysis of Development Studies, see A. M. M. Hoogvelt: The Sociology of Developing Societies (London: Macmillan, 1978) and Higgott, op. cit.

7. Such an approach is noticeable in the academic discussion of totalitarianism at this time, particularly the work of C. J. Friedrich, "The Unique Character in Totalitarian Society" in C. J. Friedrich (ed.): Totalitarianism (Cambridge, Mass., 1954).

8. For an overview of structural functionalism and modernisation theory in sociology see Hoogvelt, op. cit., Chs. 1-3. Also T. Parsons: The Social System

(London: Routledge and Kegan Paul, 1951); E. Hagen: On the Theory of Social Change (Illinois: Dorsey Press, 1962); S. N. Eisenstadt, "Social Change, Differentiation and Evolution", American Sociological Review, 29 (1964).

9. D. Apter: Ghana in Transition (Princeton: Princeton University Press, 1957); G. Almond and J. Coleman (eds.): The Politics of Developing Areas (Princeton: Princeton University Press, 1960); G. Almond and S. Verba, The Civic Culture (Boston: Little, Brown, 1963).

10. For a further discussion of the demise of the liberal democratic model at this time see also, P. Worsley: The Third World (London: Weidenfeld, 1964).

11. A. Zolberg: Creating Political Order: The Party States of West Africa (Chicago: Chicago University Press, 1966), S. P. Huntington: Political Order in Changing Societies (New Haven: Yale University Press, 1968).

12. A. G. Frank: Sociology of Development and the Underdevelopment of Sociology (London: Pluto, 1971); and Capitalism and Underdevelopment in Latin America (New York: Monthly Review Press, 1967) Ch. 1.

13. See for example W. Rodney: How Europe Underdeveloped Africa (London: Bogel Ouverture, 1972); H. Bernstein, "Modernisation Theory and the Sociological Study of Development", Journal of Development Studies, 7 (2), 141-160; H. Magdoff; The Age of Imperialism (New York: Monthly Review Press, 1969). The influence of Frank's thesis is especially noticeable in the fortunes of P. Baran's Political Economy of Growth (New York: Monthly Review Press) which although originally published in 1957 did not achieve major impact as a 'dependency theory' until the late 1960s debate stimulated by Frank.

14. Frank, Capitalism and Underdevelopment, Ch. 1.

15. S. Amin: Unequal Development (London: Harvester, 1976); A. Emmanuel: Unequal Exchange: a Study of the Imperialism of Trade (London: New Left Books, 1972).

16. Notable in this regard were the studies of the military in Latin America; see for instance R. First: The Barrel of a Gun (London: Allen Lane, 1971).

17. L. Binder et al., Crisis and Sequences in Political Development (Princeton: Princeton University Press, 1971); D. Apter: Choice and the Politics of Allocation (New Haven: Yale University Press, 1971).

18. R. L. Rothstein: The Weak in the World of the Strong; the Developing Countries in the International System (New York: Columbia University Press, 1977); G. A. Almond and B. J. Powell: Comparative Politics: System, Process and Policy (Boston: Little, Brown, 1978).

19. W. Brandt et al., North-South: a Programme for Survival (London: Pan, 1980); P. Bauer: Dissent on Development (London: Heinemann, 1976), and Equality, the Third World and Economic Delusion (Harvard University Press, 1981).

20. B. Warren, "Imperialism and Capitalist Industrialisation", New Left Review, 81.3 44; (1973); F. H. Cordoso, "Associated Dependent Development: Theoretical and Practical Implications" in A. H. Stepan (ed.): Authoritarian Brazil (New Haven: Yale University Press, 1973). Writers such as Warren pointed out that, contrary to the general expectations of early dependency theory, a number of states at the periphery were capable of growth and structural improvement within an international capitalist environment. Above all, perhaps, such studies advocated a more specific approach to the study of development in which

a state's individual 'attributes' such as climate and natural resources should be recognised as limiting factors on a universal dependency theory.

21. I. Wallerstein: The Modern World System (London: Academic Press, 1974); and The Capitalist World Economy (Cambridge: Cambridge University Press, 1979).

22. A. Brewer, op. cit.

23. E. Laclau, "Feudalism and Capitalism in Latin America", New Left Review, 67 (1971).

24. J. Banaji, "Modes of production in a materialist conception of history", Capital and Class 3 (1977).

25. J. Petras, "New Perspectives on Imperialism and Social Classes in the Periphery" in P. Limqueco and B. MacFarlane (eds.): Neo-Marxist Theories of Development (London: Croom Helm, 1983).

26. See also A. Foster-Carter, "Marxism and Dependency Theory: a Polemic", Millenium 8 (3), 214-34; "The Modes of Production Controversy", New Left Review, 107 (1978), 47-77; "From Rostow to Gunder Frank: Conflicting Paradigms in the Analysis of Underdevelopment', World Development, 4 (3), 167-180; I. Roxborough, Theories of Underdevelopment (London: Macmillan, 1979); R. A. Higgott, op. cit.

27. R. Cohen, "The Sociology of Development and the Development of Sociology", Social Science Teacher, 12, 2 (1983).

28. R. A. Higgott, op. cit.; A. M. M. Hoogvelt, op. cit.

29. Third World Studies, U204, Open University.

30. A similar point is made by Cohen, op. cit.

SELECT BIBLIOGRAPHY

H. Alavi and T. Shanin (eds.): Introduction to the Sociology of Developing Societies (London: Macmillan, 1982).

H. Bernstein: "Modernisation Theory and the Sociological Study of Development", Journal of Development Studies, 7 (2): 1971, 141-160.

H. Bernstein (ed.): Underdevelopment and Development (Harmondsworth: Penguin, 1973).

J. Blondel: The Discipline of Politics (London: Butterworths, 1981).

A. Brewer: Marxist Theories of Imperialism (London: Routledge and Kegan Paul, 1982).

R. Cohen, "The Sociology of Development and the Development of Sociology", Social Science Teacher, 12, 2 (1983).

A. Foster-Carter, "Neo-Marxist Approaches to Development and Underdevelopment" in E. De Kadt and G. Williams (eds.); Sociology and Development (London: Tavistock, 1974).

A. G. Frank: The Sociology of Development and the Underdevelopment of Sociology (London: Pluto Press, 1971).

A. G. Frank: Capitalism and Underdevelopment in Latin America (New York: Monthly Review Press, 1969).

R. A. Higgott: Political Development Theory (London: Croom Helm, 1983).

160

A. M. M. Hoogvelt: The Sociology of Developing Societies (London: Macmillan, 1976).

S. P. Huntington: Political Order in Changing Societies (New Haven: Yale University Press, 1968).

P. Limqueco and B. MacFarlane (eds.): Neo-Marxist Theories of Development (London: Croom Helm, 1983).

T. Parsons: The Social System (London: Routledge and Kegan Paul, 1951).

I. Roxborough: Theories of Underdevelopment (London: Macmillan, 1979).

J. Taylor: From Modernisation to Modes of Production (London: Macmillan, 1979).

I. Wallerstein: The Modern World System (New York: Academic Press, 1974).

For specialist periodicals, see Peter Burnell, 'Development Studies in The Third World: A Guide to the Periodicals', Teaching Politics, Volume 13 (1984) 344-354.

Political Methodology

Martin Harrop

There are two main ways of relating the specific subject of Political Methodology to the broader discipline of Political Science. The first and probably more popular approach is to regard the study of methods as a sub-field in its own right, complete with its own arcane language and esoteric concerns. Though this interpretation in one sense acknowledges the importance of methodology, it does so in an 'arms-length' fashion. Methodologists are given their own corner in which to examine advanced and indeed incomprehensible statistical models but it is not to be expected that such games will have any impact on the serious studies conducted by mainstream political scientists. The second approach, by contrast, views methodology in terms of the service role it can perform for the rest of the discipline, advising researchers on the eclectic but not especially advanced techniques routinely used in political investigations. According to this conception, the function of the methodologist is to advise the political scientist on such useful if unglamorous matters as: how to conduct a background interview with a journalist or politician; how to perform a content analysis of party manifestos; or how to work out whether credence can be attached to a set of statistics.

Now these two approaches are by no means incompatible. Methodologists would obviously need to engage in technical debate about research techniques even if their main function were to be an advisory one. Nonetheless, I do feel that Political Science and Political Methodology have drifted apart in the post-war years in a manner beneficial to neither. On the one hand, research reports often exhibit glaring technical weaknesses while methodologists, on the other hand, certainly need to demonstrate greater sensitivity to the problems faced by researchers in the real world. Accordingly, my approach in this contribution will not be to review the latest fashions in statistics but will be to consider some recent examples of, and reflections on, the major techniques used by political scientists in their normal workaday activities.

POLITICAL METHODOLOGY AND THE BEHAVIOURAL REVOLUTION

First, however, we must place political methodology in the context of the behavioural revolution which shook Political Science in the 1950s and 1960s. The new currents in the social sciences which had been stimulated by the demands of war exerted a particular influence on Political Science in the United States where dissatisfaction with constitution − and institution − centred modes of analysis was already acute.[1] As it developed in America, the behavioural approach emphasised explanation rather than description or evaluation; the study of individuals rather than institutions; comparison rather than case-study; quantitative rather than qualitative evidence; and the similarities rather than the differences between Political Science and other social sciences. The exemplar of this new mood was Almond and Verba's *The Civic Culture,* an investigation into the conditions of democratic stability through a survey of attitudes to politics in five countries.[2] As behaviouralism became the dominant paradigm among the leading researchers in many prestigious University departments, Political Methodology emerged as a distinct sub-field within the discipline.

The British response to all this was distinctly cooler. Though political scientists here were quick to understand and even quicker to criticise the new American studies, there was no general flowering of behavioural research conducted in the United Kingdom.[3] Behaviouralism received considerable acceptance as *a* legitimate mode of enquiry but rarely was it presented as *the* approach to follow. When combined with the smaller scale of the discipline and a diffuse distrust of professionalism here, this meant that Political Methodology did not − and perhaps has still not − become an institutionalised part of the discipline in Britain. At postgraduate and more especially the undergraduate levels, methodological training is still haphazard and informal. Even now, there is much sympathy with the spirit behind Malinowski's description of his approach to field-work in anthropology: 'Behave like a gentleman, keep off the women, take quinine daily and play it by ear.'

The virtues of resisting fashion become apparent when fashions change. The 1970s witnessed a diffusion of post-behavioural ideas in American Political Science, reflecting some disenchantment with the philosophical basis, ideological emphases and practical results of behaviouralism. At the philosophical level, the enthusiasm of the behavioural pioneers for a 'science of politics' does now appear naïve.

People cannot be studied by the political scientist in the same way that a physicist examines particles: humans give meaning to their actions, they learn from their previous behaviour and the same people have even been known to behave differently in similar conditions. Whatever the theoretical possibilities of a science of politics, it would surely be imprudent for Political Science to emulate wholeheartedly the procedures of the natural sciences.[4] At the ideological level, the behavioural approach has been criticised for its emphasis on those relatively trivial aspects of politics, notably elections and public opinion, which are most easily quantified. The question, argue the critics, is not why elections are won or lost but whether they matter at all. And *this* question is not easily answered in a behavioural way.[5] The practical critique is perhaps the most persuasive of all: it is simply that behaviouralism has failed to deliver the goods. A quarter of a century on from the first calls to the behavioural banners, a science of politics still seems as far away as ever. Though the achievements of behavioural research are far from negligible when judged against more modest but realistic standards, the time nonetheless does seem ripe for a more eclectic and less evangelical approach to Political Methodology than can comfortably be accommodated in a narrow behavioural framework.

The main techniques available to political scientists are:[6]

Observation Studies	— what people do in naturally occurring politics.
Interviews and Surveys	— what people say they do in, or think about, politics.
Content Analysis	— what people record about politics.
Experiments	— what people do in artificially created politics.

Each of these methods strikes its own balance between two fundamental but incompatible desiderata of political research: first, that the technique should be capable of generating information of direct relevance to politics and, secondly, that the technique should give the researcher maximum control over what information is collected. The first criterion is about politics, the second about science. Observation studies, for example, trade off rigour in data collection and analysis for relevance to the stuff of politics. Experiments, on the other hand, maintain analytical purity at the cost of a substantial and sometimes complete loss of relevance. Though each of these methods is discussed individually below, the mark of the skilful researcher is the ability to combine techniques so that cross-checks are built into an overall strategy. Thus, hypotheses formulated on the basis of observation can be tested and refined in the laboratory; or statements made by politicians can be checked against the documentary record.

Observation Studies

The proportion of research reports based on direct observation of politics is astonishingly small given that this is often the most logical point at which to start. To a large extent, of course, this reflects the nature of the discipline; politics may be a public affair but the business is largely conducted in private. It is easier for an anthropologist to study marriage ceremonies among the Trobriand Islanders, or for a sociologist to study hooliganism on the football terraces, than it is for the political scientist to observe decision-making in Cabinet committees. Yet surely more work could be done along the lines of Richard Fenno's prize-winning study of how American Congressmen perceive and behave in their home districts.[7] Between 1970-6, Fenno made 36 visits to the constituencies of 18 different members of the House of Representatives — talking, observing and participating as he went. On the basis of this research, Fenno was able to show how strategic, contextual and personal factors interlock to produce a Congressman's 'home style'. The result was fresh light cast upon old issues of political representation.

Though observation techniques have not been systematised to any great extent, a broad distinction can be drawn between participant and non-participant observation. In the former case, the researcher adopts the 'insider' role, sharing the experiences of the subjects in the study. Participant observation can itself take the *complete* form, in which the observer would have participated in the activity even if not engaged in academic study, or the *active* form, where the participation would not have occurred naturally. Erving Goffman's incisive, entertaining and perhaps even significant discussions of the 'micro-order' of American social life provide the most fashionable examples of complete participant observation.[8] Goffman considers such apparently trivial questions as: what rules do pedestrians follow in order to avoid colliding? How do cinema-goers distribute themselves in a theatre with more seats than patrons? A far cry from the study of constitutions, certainly, but it can be argued that Goffman's work reflects a coherent view of social and political reality, a view which sees the social order as a product of implicit negotiation between ordinary people.

In less esoteric vein, reports by politicians of their own experiences provide further examples of complete participant observation. It is unfortunate here that the skills of the politician are very different from those of the political scientist. Former Oxford don he may have been, but Crossman's *Diaries* are hardly a model of cool detachment.[9] Nonetheless, the political autobiography is our equivalent of the anthropologist's fieldwork though such works need to be read critically and with a sharp eye for what is implied or even left unsaid.[10]

Active participant observation is the more traditional form of observation study. Though politics is not its primary concern, W. F. Whyte's classic study of *Street Corner Society,* based on close observation of the corner-boys of Eastern City, USA, provides a good introduction to the area. Whyte includes a useful account of the problems encountered when the researcher (in this case a white, Harvard-educated upper middle-class liberal) comes from a different social background from his subjects. These problems were even more acute in Elliot Liebow's *Tally's Corner,* a more recent but equally well-regarded study by a white sociologist of unemployed black men in Washington, D.C.

The contrast between participant and non-participant observation is best drawn in terms of the kinds rather than the quality of data produced by each method. The researcher who adopts the 'insider' role generally develops a 'feel' for the subject and an awareness of the cultural complexity of micro-politics. The 'outsider', on the other hand, is more likely to remain aware of the theoretical significance of his study and is less likely to become involved in ethical difficulties arising from the conflicting roles of observer and participant. However, it is interesting to note that many scholars who begin their research with an 'outsider' design end up as participants in the subject of their study. Richard Fenno found in his study of Congressmen that by proffering professional advice on questionnaire design to local party officials he ended up attending meetings to which he would not have been invited had he remained the quiet outsider. Paradoxically, the observer who blends into a social situation by adopting a recognised role within it may be less obtrusive, and hence produce less artificial behaviour in his subjects, than the researcher who remains a 'fly-on-the-wall'.

Most observation studies are technically unreliable; there is no assurance that a different researcher employing the same means to study the same phenomenon would end up with the same conclusions. Structured observation attempts to meet this objection by using a formal scheme for assigning units of behaviour to a set of categories. The most well-known classification of this kind is Bales' Interaction

Process Analysis, a classification which rests on the assumption that any communication within a small group can be regarded as either task-oriented or group-oriented.[11] Other coding schemes can be developed for the particular purpose at hand as in Dawe's study of quarrels among pre-school children or Katz, Goldston and Benjamin's study of productivity in bi-racial work groups in the United States.[12] Structured observation techniques are most often used as an adjunct to small group experiments, where the researcher controls the environment within which the group operates and the tasks which it is set.

My limited experience of teaching observation techniques to university students has not proved very successful. Students certainly enjoy reading the monographs but appear to have difficulty in producing a respectable ethnography of political situations with which they themselves are familiar. It may be that good ethnography consists of the implicit contrast of the culture under study with the 'home' culture and that this task is beyond the ability of young people still learning about their own culture. But the potential importance of observation studies to the political scientist justifies persistence here.

Interviews and Surveys

Though structured questionnaires administered to the general public are one of the most public (and expensive) manifestations of Political Methodology, the typical interview conducted by a political researcher is probably an informal, background conversation with another member of the elite, whether politician, journalist, bureaucrat or other researcher. Often indeed such interviews will serve as a primary if wholly indirect source for a description of behaviour as well as attitudes. For instance, Heclo and Wildavsky's description of 'the Whitehall village' is based largely on interviews with Ministers and civil servants even though it is written up in a quasi-observational way.[13] The Nuffield election studies also rely substantially though not exclusively on interviews in order to reconstruct the logic (or lack of it) underlying political behaviour in the election campaign.[14] As with participant observation, the skills required to conduct a successful elite interview are not easily taught or even well-understood. It is clear, however, that the fundamental skill required for unstructured interviewing is the ability to develop rapport with the respondent without engaging in self-disclosure which might bias the answers. This calls for interpersonal skills which are more likely to develop in the field than in the library — though Gorden's American text is at least a comprehensive guide to interviewing techniques.[1 5]

Philip Williams' reflections on the more than 300 interviews he conducted in preparing his biography of Hugh Gaitskell are one of the few British contributions to the art of elite interviewing in politics.[1 6] In comparison to Gorden's text, Williams' comments are atheoretical and intuitive but also succinct and interesting. It is intriguing to note, for instance, that Williams appears to have arrived by himself at what is emerging as a generally accepted conclusion about the undesirability of tape recording interviews:

> Rightly or wrongly, I used a tape-recorder only once, in the very first interview of all. An old acquaintance of Gaitskell's, whom I knew slightly, was leaving for Australia. I had not used the machines before, and took one along as an experiment; my informant was familiar with them and had no objection, and as I switched it on I could see him square his shoulders – literally – to Speak for History.

Williams also raises the uncomfortable question: why should we believe what people tell us in interviews? As with any other research technique, valid findings are equated with results which survive attempts at falsification. Thus, the transcript of an interview can be checked for internal consistency and for consistency with other interviews and the documentary record. If there are no apparent reasons for the respondent not to tell the truth (and in politics this is a pretty big if), any finding which survives these checks can be provisionally accepted. But even this procedure begins, in Williams' words, 'with the simple and charitable assumption that on the whole people will seek to tell you the truth.' The cynic who rejects even this assumption would forestall the possibility of error – but at the unacceptable cost of removing any chance of arriving at the truth.

Structured questionnaires administered to samples of the general public, or indeed any other group, obviously differ in style and content from the semi-structured, elite interviews conducted by Williams. But although survey work tends to be regarded as a model of behavioural research in Political Science, it is important to recognise that surveys are a most inappropriate methodology for answering certain types of questions. It would be unwise to rely solely on survey data when the factors under study can be varied experimentally; when the primary focus is behaviour rather than opinion; or when the unit of analysis is the individual rather than the variable – that is, when one is interested in people 'in the round'. Surveys are however appropriate for answering descriptive questions (*how many* people believe Denis Healey is a

Conservative?); questions about the factors, whether causal or not, which distinguish one group from another (*what kinds of people* believe Healey is a Conservative?); and especially questions about trends (do *more or less* people now believe Healey is a Conservative than did so when he was Chancellor?). Our capacity to answer questions such as these with a known degree of precision on the basis of properly drawn samples of about a thousand undoubtedly gives modern political scientists an enormous advantage over previous generations of scholars.

The major controversy within the academic community about survey research is whether questionnaires impose a 'structure of meaning' on respondents who may think about the relevant issues in very different terms from the researcher. This critique has been taken furthest in Sociology, where greater stress is laid upon seeing the world from the respondent's point of view.[17] Yet this criticism is more accurately applied to inadequate applications of survey research than to the method itself. A well-designed questionnaire results from extensive pilot work which serves to establish, if only in general terms, the extent, style and content of respondents' thinking on the topic under investigation.[18] It is only when this preliminary stage is skimped (as it often has to be with opinion polls conducted under pressure of time for the media) that surveys are in danger of becoming an exercise in miscommunication, with well-educated, middle-class and highly informed researchers asking over-sophisticated questions of poorly-educated, working-class respondents who know little and care less about the subject in question.

Interview-based projects, using structured or unstructured designs, obviously form an essential element in teaching interviewing skills. Video recording of dummy interviews is, where possible, a particularly effective way of increasing students' self-awareness. However, projects of this kind often work best if a structured questionnaire is the end-product rather than the starting-point of the project. Although there is no reason why a project should not replicate the pilot research involved in a full-scale, professional survey, it is not always practical for a student project to achieve a respectable sample size. The disadvantage of qualitative projects, though, is that students are not able to engage in statistical analysis of the information collected. This is a significant drawback when the institution has access to a computer, for statistical programmes are now available which can be learnt (and taught!) by people who have no idea about the internal workings of a computer.[19]

Content Analysis

Most political research involves the analysis of documents of various kinds, whether as primary or supplementary material. The objective, systematic and quantitative description of such information is content analysis, a crude and somewhat unfashionable technique which nonetheless still has its place in the political scientist's methodology armoury.[20] Content analysis is essentially a data-reduction technique — a method of disposing of all the information in a communication except that which is central to the research purpose. This aim is achieved by reducing words to numbers.

Content analysis should not be equated with word counts by computers. Though computers can be of value, content analysis is more often conducted by trained researchers who code whatever is the most appropriate unit of analysis for a given project: the sentence, paragraph, page or chapter. In her study of changes in women's status in American magazine fiction, for example, Cornella Flora coded 202 short stories according to the extent of passivity shown by the female characters appearing in them.[21] Even though the entire story served as the unit of analysis, inter-coder reliability was more than 95%.

What results can be obtained from content analysis which would not emerge from simply reading the material? At the most general and probably least important level, the principal gain is replicability; the procedures involved can be fully described and the accuracy of the findings checked by other researchers. More specifically, content analysis can perform two functions which at the very least supplement a qualitative interpretation. First, it can sometimes help to solve problems of disputed authorship. When it is not known whether X or Y wrote a document, samples of X's writing can be compared with Y's to find the elements of style which most clearly discriminate between the two authors. The classic example here is Mosteller and Wallace's elegant solution to a problem which had puzzled many generations of historians: was Alexander Hamilton or James Madison the author of 12 of the 85 Federalist Papers whose authorship could not be definitely established by orthodox historical methods?[22] After much fruitless work, the researchers established that Hamilton employed the words 'enough' and 'upon' far more frequently than Madison. Hamilton also wrote 'while' where Madison would use 'whilst'. The disputed papers matched Madison's literary fingerprint much more closely than Hamilton's. At the very least, this exercise confirmed the belief already held by most contemporary historians that Madison was indeed the

170

author of the documents in question.

The second advantage of content analysis is that it allows the investigator to compare more material than could be grasped in raw form by a single mind. Child, Storm and Veroff, for example, examined the relationship between 'need for achievement' and a number of other psychological variables revealed in an analysis of 12 folk tales for each of 46 societies.[23] A qualitative assessment of such a vast body of material would not really have been practical. More recently, David Robertson has attempted to test theories of party competition by examining the content of British party manifestos between 1924 and 1966.[24] This material totals many thousands of words. By virtue of its data-reduction function, then, content analysis can increase the researcher's span though at some cost in terms of depth of interpretation.

There is no difficulty in constructing practical exercises for use in teaching content analysis. By asking students to independently code the same material into categories predetermined by the instructor, a ready measure of inter-coder reliability is obtained. I have asked students to code the articles in extremist publications according to the primary political target of the report, an exercise which usually leads at least some students to reassess the impressions they formed of the journal in an initial qualitative reading.

Experiments

Experiments are the ideal basis from which to analyse the causal relations between variables. Even in a discipline such as Political Science where experimental manipulation of variables is often impossible or impractical, the experimental method nonetheless provides an important reference point for assessing the inadequacies of less pure if more realistic research designs. The difficulties notwithstanding, an increasing number of experiments are being conducted in political studies and we may expect this growth to continue.

The logic of a simple experiment is:

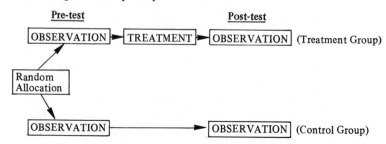

This illustrates the two fundamental features of much experimental work: first, the use of a control group and, secondly, the random allocation of individuals to the treatment group or the control group. A control group consists of subjects who are identical to those in the treatment group except that they are not given the 'treatment' whose effects are the subject of enquiry. Random assignment to one of the two groups is needed to ensure that the two groups are indeed as similar as possible. With research on human subjects, this can create ethical difficulties where the treatment might prove to be beneficial, or more rarely, harmful. Nonetheless, given a design of the kind shown in the figure, the effects of the treatment can be determined by comparing post-test observations on the two groups with the pre-test situation.[25]

One of the first experiments to receive widespread attention in Political Science was Stanley Milgram's controversial study of obedience to authority.[26] He examined the amount of electric shock a subject was willing to give another person when asked to do so by a confederate of the experimenter. The subject believed the purpose of the project was to determine the effect of punishment on memory and was not aware that the 'victim' was in fact feigning pain from the 'shock'. It transpired that many subjects were willing to give a shock described as 'danger: severe shock' on the 'shock generator'; this was particularly likely when the subject could not hear, see or most especially touch the 'victim'. In one sense, the subjects were the real victims of this study for the belief that they were administering pain itself caused them substantial stress. This experiment would not now pass the stricter ethical standards which were introduced partly as a result of Milgram's study.[27]

Discussion of Milgram's work has centred on the applicability of his results to real situations. This issue of *external validity* is a recurring problem in laboratory work; it is often not at all clear whether the findings can be generalised to other populations and settings, particularly when social science students provide the subjects. The obvious solution to this problem is to take the experimental method into the field, as in Bochel and Denver's study of canvassing, turnout and party support.[28] These authors exposed the residents of a block of council flats in Dundee to a sustained canvas during a local election in 1970 and then compared turnout with a 'control' block which had received no canvassing. The results showed that contrary to the conventional wisdom of political scientists if not party activists, canvassing not only increased turnout but also indirectly increased Labour's share of the vote.

Yet the artificiality of most experiments is in some ways a strength rather than a weakness. It is possible in the laboratory to observe the reactions of people to situations which do not now exist but might do so in the future and hence gain some insight into the desirability of bringing such circumstances to fruition. For example, would it make any difference to decision-making if key political decisions were made by women rather than men? Given the male domination of most polities, controlled comparisons of decisions made by all-male and all-female groups in constructed situations are one of the few sources of information on this topic.[29] Similar reasoning lies behind the efforts occasionally made by students of international relations to answer that grand historical question 'what if?' by first reconstructing historical situations in a simulation and then altering the course of 'history' to test the effect of one particular factor on subsequent events.[30]

The New Jersey Graduated Work Incentive Experiment is the major example of a field experiment designed to cast light on a 'what if?' question though in this case the question was posed by policy-makers rather than historians.[31] The question was: would the provision by the State of a guaranteed income to poor families reduce the incentive to work? One thousand three hundred and fifty families in New Jersey and Pennsylvania were given one of four levels of guaranteed income, ranging from 50% to 125% of the official poverty level. Labour market participation by husbands in the families receiving payment proved to be no less than that of husbands in a control group though the wives on average worked 23% fewer hours. Though experiments of this kind are a tremendously valuable technique for the evaluation of options facing governments, political criteria will of course remain predominant in the decision-making process as long as it is politicians who make policy. The sting in the tail of the New Jersey experiment, for instance, is that the Nixon administration put forward its own guaranteed income plan in 1969 before even the preliminary results of the experiment were made available, under pressure, in 1970.

Experiments, then, have an important role to play in most empirical disciplines, politics included. There is no doubt that political scientists could incorporate experiments into their projects more often and more creatively than they do so at present. Teaching experimental design is also a straight-forward matter since the basic principles are extremely simple and any class of students can provide both the organisers of and the subjects for an experiment.[32]

CONCLUSION

This review of the principal techniques used in political research reflects the methodological eclecticism of the discipline. Political Science is quite rightly defined by its subject matter rather than its methodology. Furthermore, the same techniques can be used for very different strategic purposes — to test a general theory of politics, to use a theory in the understanding of a particular case or, more often, to do a little of both. In the post-behavioural era, there is no longer any reason to regard this situation of intellectual pluralism as indefensible or even undesirable. The use of multiple methods is the surest way of discovering which apparent 'results' are an artefact of technique. Besides, it is surely important for the development of the profession that researchers should work with those techniques which they are most competent to employ. But one consequence of this heterogeneity is that the research reports appearing in the journals offer a bewildering array of methods — and of methodological sophistication. To the untutored eye, and sometimes even to the tutored one, pluralism can appear as confusion. Yet the impulse to tidy the field should be resisted. Political Methodology, like politics itself, is inherently a confusing business.

• NOTES

1. An influential war-time work was S. Stouffer et. al.: The American Soldier (Princeton: University Press, 2 Volumes, 1949).

2. For an update, see G. Almond and S. Verba (eds.): The Civic Culture Revisited (Boston: Little, Brown, 1980).

3. B. Crick's The American Science of Politics (Berkeley: University of California Press, 1959) was an early British critique of the behavioural approach. For a much sharper analysis by a British political scientist of particular behavioural works, see B. Barry: Sociologists, Economists and Democracy (Chicago: University of Chicago Press, 1978).

4. A. Ryan's The Philosophy of the Social Sciences (London: Macmillan, 1970) is an excellent review of the philosophical issues involved here.

5. See for example G. Graham and G. Carey (eds.): The Post-Behavioural Era: Perspectives on Political Science (Chicago: McKay, 1972).

6. This list is adapted from J. A. Banks, 'Sociological Theories, Methods and Research Techniques', Sociological Review, Volume 27 (1978), 561-78.

7. R. Fenno: Home Style: House Members in Their Districts (Boston: Little, Brown, 1978).

8. Good examples of Goffman's style are: Relations in Public (London: Allen Lane, 1971) and Interaction Ritual (Harmondsworth: Penguin, 1972). For a review, see J. Ditton: The View from Goffman (London: Macmillan, 1980).

9. Nor, to be fair, were they intended to be. The reflections of a non-elected Minister who has now returned to politics teaching are found in P. Kellner and Lord Crowther-Hunt: The Civil Servants: An Inquiry into Britain's Ruling Class (London: Macdonald, 1980).

10. Though G. Kaufmann's How To Be A Minister (London: Sidgwick and Jackson, 1980) strikes a more observant tone than many books by politicians.

11. R. Bales: Interaction Process Analysis (Chicago: University Press, 1951).

12. Both cited in C. Sellitz et. al.: Research Methods in Social Relations (London: Methuen, 1965), Ch. 6.

13. H. Heclo and A. Wildavsky: The Private Government of Public Money (Berkeley: University of California Press, 1974).

14. For the most recent book in the series, see D. Butler and D. Kavanagh: The British General Election of 1979 (London: Macmillan, 1980).

15. R. Gorden: Interviewing: Strategy, Techniques and Tactics (Homewood: Dorsey, 1980). An earlier work by a political scientist is L. Dexter: Elite and Specialised Interviewing (Evanston: Northwestern University Press, 1970).

16. Philip Williams, 'Interviewing Politicians: The Life of Hugh Gaitskell', Political Quarterly, Volume 51 (1980), 303-16.

17. See, for example, A. Cicourel: Method and Measurement in Sociology, (New York: Free Press, 1964) and Cognitive Sociology (Harmondsworth: Penguin, 1973).

18. A good, non-technical guide to the various stages of a survey is G. Hoinville, R. Jowell and Associates: Survey Research Practice (London: Heinemann, 1978). C. Moser and G. Kalton: Survey Methods in Social Investigation (London: Heinemann, 1971) is more comprehensive but also more difficult. S. Payne's The Art of Asking Questions (Princeton: University Press, 1951) remains the best and most readable book on questionnaire construction.

19. Most issues of the journal Behaviour Research: Methods and Instrumentation contain details of programmes of this kind. Before obtaining any programme, technical advice is needed to ensure that the programme can run on the make and model of computer to which you have access. For advice, consult the sources on p. 619 of the Education Year Book 1981 (London: Councils and Education Press, 1980).

20. The definition is from B. Berelson: Content Analysis in Communication Research (New York: Hafner Press, 1971).

21. C. Flora, 'Changes in Women's Status in Women's Magazine Fiction', Social Problems, Volume 26 (1979), 558-69.

22. F. Mosteller and D. Wallace: Inference and Disputed Authorship: The Federalist (Reading, Mass: Addison-Wesley, 1964).

23. Reported in J. Atkinson (ed.): Motives in Fantasy, Action and Society (Princeton: Van Nostrand, 1958), 479-93. This built on the work of D. McClelland et. al.: The Achievement Motive (New York: Appleton-Century-Crofts, 1953).

24. D. Robertson: A Theory of Party Competition (London: Wiley, 1976).

25. D. Campbell and J. Stanley: Experimental and Quasi-Experimental

Designs for Research (Chicago: Rand McNally, 1963) is a lucid introduction.

26. S. Milgram: Obedience to Authority (New York: Harper and Row, 1975). A film of the experiment can be hired from the Scottish Central Film Library, 74 Victoria Crescent Road, Dowanhill, Glasgow G12 9JN.

27. For a review of the ethical issues involved in social research, both experimental and field-based, see P. Reynolds: Ethical Dilemmas and Social Science Research (San Francisco: Jossey-Bass, 1979).

28. J. Bochel and D. Denver, 'Canvassing, Turnout, and Party Support', British Journal of Political Science, Volume 1 (1971), 257-69.

29. For a review of sex differences in strategies followed in laboratory games, see V. Sapiro, 'Sex and Games: On Oppression and Rationality', British Journal of Political Science, Volume 9 (1979), 385-408.

30. For example, C. and M. Hermann, 'An Attempt to Simulate the Outbreak of World War I', American Political Science Review, Volume 61 (1967), 400-16.

31. H. Watts and A. Rees (eds.): The New Jersey Income Tax Maintenance Experiment (Washington: Academic Press, 1977, three volumes).

32. Useful aids are: C. Ward: Laboratory Manual in Experimental Social Psychology (New York: Holt, Rinehart and Winston, 1970) or, in lighter vein, M. Laver: Playing Politics (Harmondsworth: Penguin, 1981).

SELECT BIBLIOGRAPHY

R. Bernstein and J. Dyer: An Introduction to Political Science Methods (Englewood Cliffs: Prentice-Hall, 1979).

D. Campbell and J. Stanley: Experimental and Quasi-Experimental Designs for Research (Chicago: Rand McNally 1963).

A. Cicourel: Method and Measurement in Sociology (New York: Free Press, 1964).

L. Dexter: Elite and Specialised Interviewing (Evanston: Northwestern University Press, 1970).

J. Ditton, ed.: The View from Goffman (London: Macmillan, 1980).

R. Fenno: Home Style: House Members in their Districts (Boston: Little, Brown, 1978).

G. Graham and G. Carey, eds.: The Post-Behavioural Era: Perspectives on Political Science (Chicago: McKay, 1972).

F. Greenstein and N. Polsby, eds.: Handbook of Political Science Volume 7: Strategies of Enquiry (Reading, Mass.: Addison-Wesley, 1975).

G. Hoinville, R. Jowell and Associates: Survey Research Practice (London: Heinemann, 1978).

O. Holsti: Content Analysis for the Social Sciences and Humanities (Reading, Mass.: Addison-Wesley, 1969).

M. Laver: Playing Politics (Harmondsworth: Penguin, 1981).

D. Leege and W. Francis: Political Research: Design, Measurement and Analysis (New York: Basic Books, 1974).

G. McCall and J. Simmons: Issues in Participant Observation (Reading, Mass.: Addison-Wesley, 1969).

S. Payne: The Art of Asking Questions (Princeton: University Press, 1951).

N. Polsky: Hustlers, Beats and Others (Garden City, N.Y.: Anchor Books, 1969).

P. Reynolds: Ethical Dilemmas and Social Science Research (San Francisco: Jossey-Bass, 1979).

W. Runciman: Social Science and Political Theory (Cambridge: University Press, 1963).

A. Ryan: The Philosophy of the Social Sciences (London: Macmillan, 1970).

A. Somit and J. Tanenhaus: The Development of American Political Science: From Burgess to Behaviouralism (New York: Irvington, 1980).

P. Winch: The Idea of a Social Science and its Relation to Philosophy (Atlantic Highlands, N.J.: Humanities Press, 1970).

CONTRIBUTORS

Neil Casey, Plymouth Polytechnic

Alex Cunliffe, Plymouth Polytechnic

Michael Goldsmith, University of Salford

Chris Goodrich, formerly University of Manchester now with the National Federation of Housing Associations

Rod Hague, The University of Newcastle Upon Tyne

Martin Harrop, The University of Newcastle Upon Tyne

Roger King, Huddersfield Polytechnic

Alan Lawton, Teesside Polytechnic

Lynton Robins, Leicester Polytechnic

Graham E. Smith, Cambridge University

Steve Smith, University of East Anglia

Neville C. Woodhead, Leicester Polytechnic

David J. Wilson, Leicester Polytechnic

Index

180

Observation Studies 164-66
Offe, C. 53, 54, 57, 64
O'Laughlin, J. 141
O'Leary, M. 116
Olson, M. 40, 90
OPEC 118
Opinion polls 168

Paddison, R. 135, 136
Pahl, R. 64, 68
Panitch, L. 54
Paradigms 107-8, 110
Paris, C. 68, 70
Pareto principle 93, 137
Pareto, V. 49, 50
Parsons, T. 152
Pateman, C. 22
Pelassy, D. 33
Pennock, R. 3
Petras, J. 155
Philosophy 20-23, 107, 111, 122
Picciotto, S. 53
Pilot surveys 168
Pitt, D. 81
Plato 17, 18
Playford, J. 10
Policy-making 67-68, 114
    intended and unintended effects
        69-70
Political attitudes 51
Political business cycle 99
Political concepts 33, 34
Political Geography Quarterly 135,
    142
Political participation 49, 75, 153
Political Science
    and behaviouralism 9-11, 35, 49,
        114, 115, 116, 162, 163, 173
    and experiments 170
    and Marxism 6, 12
    and moral philosophy 5
    and political institutions 8
    and post-behaviouralism 11, 115
    and the scientific approach 6, 10,
        28, 29, 30, 92, 109, 162-63
    Western view of 12, 150
Political socialisation 49, 57
Political system 28, 35-36, 63
Politics Association 1
Politics of everyday life 3, 4
Pontin, G. 1
Positivism 94
Poulantzas, N. 53, 85

Powell, B. J. 154
Powell, G. B. 35
Power relations 47-48, 113
Pressure groups 54, 68, 133
Prince, H. 134
Prisoners' Dilemma 95
Protestant ethic 56
Psychology 35, 42, 82
Public goods 137
Public Sector 29, 81
Putnam, R. D. 39

Quangos 68, 79
Quantification 132, 141, 161
Questionnaires 166-67

Rachmanism 69
Rae, D. W. 32
Rate Support Grant 139
Ratzel, F. 126
Rawls, J. 22, 93
Reagan, R. 26
Representation 95
Revolution 53, 150
Rex, J. 56
Rhodes, R. A. W. 65, 72, 75, 87
Ridley, F. F. 8
Rigby, T. H. 27
Roberts, G. K. 29, 31
Robertson, D. 170
Robson, W. A. 81
Rockman, B. A. 39
Rokkan, S. 31, 50, 51
Rose, R. 40
Rosenthal, D. 132, 134
Ross, A. 102
Rostow, W. W. 150, 152
Rothstein, R. 113, 154
Runciman, W. 47

Salaman, L. M. 26
Sartori, G. 33, 34
Saunders, P. 56, 62, 64, 65, 70
Schmitter, P. 54
Schneider, F. 101
Schumpeter, J. 21, 50
Sen, A. 93
Sharkansky, I. 65
Sharpe, L. J. 66, 73
Short, J. 131
Singer, D. 115
Skinner, Q. 18-19
Skocpol, T. 31, 53

THE POLITICS ASSOCIATION

THE POLITICS ASSOCIATION was founded in 1969 in order to provide a professional service for those engaged or interested in the teaching of political subjects. The Association promotes the study and teaching of the theory and practice of local, national and international politics. It provides, by research, publications, meetings and courses, for continuous improvement in the quality of politics teaching.

Membership of the Association provides the opportunity to receive publications and participate in activities, all of which encourage the exchange of ideas and experiences, and which make the teacher aware of recent developments in the subject matter and the teaching of Politics. Services include:

★ *Teaching Politics,* the journal of the Politics Association. The journal includes articles on curriculum issues, updating articles on syllabus content, simulation material and detailed book reviews.

★ *The Politics Association Resources Bank* supplies up-to-date material in the form of written resources, cassette recordings and video tapes.

★ *Grass Roots,* the newsletter of the Politics Association. This includes up-to-date information on conferences, courses, branch activities, and details of television programmes of interest to the Politics teacher.

★ *Conference and branches.* The Politics Association holds an annual conference for members. In addition, the Association organises regional conferences for sixth form Politics students together with a residential revision course. The Association has a number of branches which meet regularly at regional and local level.

★ *Textbooks and Revision Aids. British Politics Today, Topics in British Politics, Updating British Politics,* and the Longman series on Political Realities are books produced by or in association with the Politics Association.

★ The *Politics PAL* revision aid is a Politics Association resource.

How to join. Send for an application form to: The Politics Association, 16 Gower Street, London WC1E 6DP.